COVIDCONOMICS
TAMING INFLATION WITHOUT
INCREASING INTEREST RATES

by LINKEDIN AND TOWN HALL ACHIEVER OF THE YEAR
EY NOMINEE ENTREPRENEUR OF THE YEAR
GRAND HOMAGE LYS DIVERSITY
WORLD TOP100 DOCTOR

Dr. BAK NGUYEN, DMD

&

CO-AUTHORS
ANDRÉ CHÂTELAIN, MBA
TRANIE VO, B. ENG.
FRANÇOIS DUFOUR, MBA, MSc
WILLIAM BAK

TO ALL CITIZENS, LEADERS, DECISION-MAKERS AND
ORGANIZATIONS WITH THE POWER TO WRITE HISTORY
par Dr. BAK NGUYEN

ISBN: 978-1-989536-97-1

Published by: Dr. BAK PUBLISHING COMPANY
Dr.BAK 0112

COVIDCONOMICS

TAMING INFLATION WITHOUT INCREASING INTEREST RATES

by Dr. BAK NGUYEN, ANDRÉ CHÂTELAIN,
TRANIE VO, FRANÇOIS DUFOUR
& WILLIAM BAK

DISCLAIMER

« The general information, opinions and advice contained in this medium and/or the books, audiobooks, podcasts and publications on Dr. Bak Nguyen, André Châtelain, Tranie Vo, François Dufour and William Bak (legal name Dr. Ba Khoa Nguyen, Lam Tra Nien Vo and William Bak Nguyen) and his collaborator's website or social media (hereinafter the "Opinions") present general information on various topics. The Opinions are intended for informational purposes only.

No information contained in the Opinions is a substitute for an expert, consultation, advice, diagnosis or professional treatment. No information contained in the Opinions is a substitute for professional advice and should not be construed as consultation or advice.

Nothing in the Opinions should be construed as professional advice related to the practice of dentistry, medical advice or any other form of advice, including legal or financial advice, professional opinion, care or diagnosis, but strictly as general information. All information from the Opinions is for informational purposes only.

Any user who disagrees with the terms of this Disclaimer should immediately cease using or referring to the Opinions. Any action by the user in connection with the information contained in the Opinions is solely at the user's discretion.

The general information contained in the Opinions is provided "as is" and without warranty of any kind, either expressed or implied. Dr. Bak Nguyen and his collaborators (André Châtelain, Tranie Vo, François Dufour and William Bak - legal name Dr. Ba Khoa Nguyen, Lam Tra Nien Vo and William Bak Nguyen) makes every effort to ensure that the information is complete and accurate. However, there is no guarantee that the general information contained in the Opinions is always available, truthful, complete, up-to-date or relevant.

ABOUT THE AUTHORS

From Canada, **Dr. BAK NGUYEN**, Nominee Ernst and Young Entrepreneur of the year, Grand Homage Lys DIVERSITY, LinkedIn & TownHall Achiever of the year and TOP 100 Doctors 2021. Dr. Bak is a cosmetic dentist, CEO and founder of Mdex & Co. His company is revolutionizing the dental field. Speaker and motivator, he holds the world record of writing 100 books in 4 years accumulating many world records (to be officialized). Before that, he held the world record of writing 9 books over 12 months, then, 15 books within 15 months to set the bar even higher with the world record of 36 books written within 18 months + 1 week.By his second author anniversary, he scored his new landmark world record of 48 books within 24 months. And then 72 books in 36 months. By the 4th anniversary, Dr. Bak scored his usual landmark of writing 96 books over 48 months, but he pushed even further, scoring also the new world record of 100 books written within 4 years!

His books are covering: ENTREPRENEURSHIP, LEADERSHIP, QUEST OF IDENTITY, DENTISTRY AND MEDICINE, PARENTING, CHILDREN BOOKS, PHILOSOPHY

In 2003, he founded Mdex, a dental company upon which in 2018, he launched the most ambitious private endeavour to reform the dental industry, Canada-wide. Philosopher, he has close to his heart the quest of happiness of the people surrounding him, patients and colleagues alike. In 2020, he launched an International collaborative initiative named **THE ALPHAS** to share knowledge between Entrepreneurs and Doctors to thrive through the Greatest Pandemic and Economic depression of our time. To support creativity and the empowerment of self-improvement and personal growth, Dr. Bak is also leading the advancement of A.I. (Artificial Intelligence) at Emotive World Incorporated. Incorporating A.I., design and publishing into its workflow and product, Emotive World is a leading company in publishing stories and books through writing and audio format. Under the leadership of Dr. Bak, Emotive World launched the Apollo Protocol, allowing authors to write books within 24 hours of working time, the Echo Protocol, to produce audiobooks like this one, to publish books distributed by Amazon, Barnes & Noble, Apple Books and Kindle and to also create and produce audiobook blockbusters, U.A.X. (Ultimate Audio Experience) streaming on Apple Music, Spotify and all major outlets.Dr. Bak with his implication in Emotive World, is vouching to empower the voice and creation of all the authors in the world to reach their markets and their audience. Yes Dr. Bak is an author, but through Emotive World, he is also a publishing and production company.
He also holds recognitions from the Canadian Parliament and the Canadian Senate.

From Canada, **ANDRÉ CHATELAIN** acts as a Business Consultant and offers coaching services for managers and senior executives. In addition, he contributes, with the Université de Sherbrooke, to the development of training programs for 2nd cycle companies and students. He also sits on a few Boards of Directors. Until September 3, 2017, he was Senior Vice-President, Personal Services, Payment and Marketing at Desjardins Group. His mandate was to develop and deploy banking and financing for retail clients, as well as payment solutions for the Desjardins group. Its teams are also responsible for marketing activities for individual clients and marketing activities for all clienteles across Quebec.

Transversally, as first vice-president, he also managed the Desjardins brand and ensured the alignment and cohesion of Desjardins' actions in terms of marketing and customers' experience in all distribution channels. Mr. Chatelain worked for Desjardins Group for 28 years During which, he held various positions in the areas of corporate finance, business development, risk management, marketing, operational efficiency and strategic planning. He has also held several management positions, including Vice-President of Risk Management, Vice-President of Marketing – Business and, more recently, Senior Vice-President and General Manager of Desjardins Card Services. Mr. Chatelain has served on several boards internally and externally with the Desjardins Group. He has a Master in Business Administration (MBA) from the Université de Sherbrooke and a Bachelor of Administration (BAA concentration finance) from the Université du Québec en Outaouais.

From Canada, **FRANÇOIS DUFOUR** has been an entrepreneur and a marketer all of his life. Throughout his career, he has always been the one asking the hard questions to himself and his contemporaries to better understand societal and economic mechanisms. He has obtained a bachelor's degree in economics from Bishop's University, a Master of Science from ESCEM-Poitiers and a master's in business (International Management) from Sherbrooke University.

From Canada, **TRANIE VO** is the co-founder and COO of Mdex & Co, a management company in the health sector. Graduated from McGill University with a Bachelor in mechanical engineering, she co-founded the company which she built from the ground up for the last 20 years. She is a veteran entrepreneur embodying woman's leadership and the diversity movement of the leader class. She co-wrote a book with her partner, Dr. Bak Nguyen on the balance to maintain between being a leader and a woman, standing behind her man. In 2020, with her determination and resilience, she inspired the creation of the international organization of thinkers and difference makers known as THE ALPHAS.

From Canada, **William Bak** is a 12 years old prodigy. At the age of 8 years old, he co-wrote a series of chicken books with his dad, Dr. Bak. Together, they are changing the world, one mind at a time, writing books for kids. So far, they have 32 books together. He co-wrote the 11 chicken books in ENGLISH and then, had to translate his own books in FRENCH. This is how he has 22 chicken books. William also co-wrote 4 parenting books with his dad, Dr. Bak, THE BOOK OF LEGENDS volumes 1, 2 and 3. The 4th volume started a new trilogy named THE RISE OF LEGENDS; the first volume of THE RISE OF LEGENDS; 2 Vaccine books (French and English); TIMING, William's first Apollo Protocol book. Lately, William has also written his first book solo at the age of 11, PAPA, J'SUIS PAS CON and the PROLOGUES OF DESTINY, volumes 1 and 2, and AU PAYS DES PAPAS 1 and 2.To promote his books, William embraced the stage for the first time in 2019 talking to a crowd of 300+ people. Since he has appeared in many videos to talk about his books and upcoming projects. In the midst of COVID, he got bored and started his YOUTUBE CHANNEL: GAMEBAK, reviewing video games. By the end of 2020, he has joined THE ALPHAS as the youngest anchor of the upcoming world project COVIDCONOMICS in which he will give his perspective and host the opinions of his generation.

"I will show you. I won't force you. But I won't wait for you."
- William Bak and Dr. Bak

Writing with his Dad, William holds world records to be officialized: the youngest author writing in 2 languages, co-author of 8 books within a month, the first kid to have written 20 children's books, the child to have written his first solo book in 9 days, the first child who wrote 36 books within 45 months.

INTRODUCTION

By Dr. BAK NGUYEN
& TRANIE VO

Greetings Alphas. Yes, I am greeting each and every single one of you as Alphas since you are reading these lines. We all have suffered a great deal through the last 2 and a half years of pandemics. Where most are tired and claiming for their dues, rights, or even wishes, we, Alphas, are looking for solutions to fix the damages of the last storm while looking ahead to avoid the next one. Whoever you are, you are one of us. You are an Alpha.

And what is an Alpha exactly? We are not pretending to be any different or any better than anyone else. What makes us special, Alphas, is that we rise to the occasion, being the first on the line, running towards the problem instead of fleeing from it. That is why, I am taking my words, leadership, and status to address you today, fellow Alphas. I am addressing you, as a concerned citizen who is trying to pull his own weight, bringing to the table his talents and powers.

I am also addressing you as an entrepreneur who withstood the storm and the flood of the last 2 years in COVID, holding the fort and leading his company while taking care of his patients. If the health professionals were our heroes and the first line of defence in the COVID war, the entrepreneurs were playing defence and are now called upon to lead the comeback.Under sieged and heavily tested, they took on their shoulders, with the help of the different governments, more and more debts to patch their ship, waiting for the storm to pass.

Well, now that we are in recovering mode, the entrepreneurial class is now our main hope and force to rebuild our economy and to heal from the 2 and a half years of pandemic. And why so much praises for the entrepreneurs? How many people do you know who are paying to work? How many people do you know who borrow and mortgage their future to put other people to work? Sure, entrepreneurs are doing so, hoping for a big return eventually but meanwhile, who are paying to work?

Forget about the wages raising and the improvement of better working conditions. Forget about the pandemic, the fatigue, and the shortage of staff. Entrepreneurs were on the line, playing defence for the last 30 months and now, we are looking up to them to lead the way back to prosperity.

"Hope and morale are the fuel of the entrepreneurs."

Dr. Bak Nguyen

They are good because they believe and they are willing to bet on themselves to lead the way. Well, the last 30 months were particularly hard on them. Many have already fallen at the front.

Now that 2 wars are raging, the Ukraine war and the Energy crisis, will these wars have reason of our entrepreneurial class? This whole book is about analysis and solutions to avoid the upcoming crisis, one that will affect each and every one of us. But allow me a few more minutes to make the case of the entrepreneurial class and the legitimacy of my involvement in this crisis.

Well, as the Pandemic stretched over the last 30 months (and we are not officially out of it yet), that has stalled the economy on many, many levels. Confinement, working remotely, curfews, and discrimination (vax and antivax) changed the landscape of life as we knew it.

My offices are located in the heart of downtown Montreal, on the Golden Square mile, which is the most prestigious district in the metropolis. Well, for the last 2 years, that was a ghost town. People were barely back for the last 4 months and even so. This is not about my case as an entrepreneur, but just to illustrate that if the economy in general has suffered, some local economy has been decimated. Montreal is not a unique case.

To survive, governments have extended many subsidies and loan programs to help our entrepreneurs. Thanks to that precious help, many enterprises have survived the pandemic only to face a new threat: the shortage of staff and the explosion of wages.

"Entrepreneurs are not people who will complain. They are too busy trying to fix the problem."

Dr. Bak Nguyen

For months and months, they faced these crises trying to make up for the difference, resisting for as long as possible to raise their price. But everyone has to face the music eventually.

Now, between the shortage of staff, the explosion in logistics costs (import-export), and the demand that is still shy to come back, a new menace is flooding each and every entrepreneurial ship: the rise of the interest rates. Sure, inflation is raising and raising fast to the point that our officials are trying their best not to say that control is lost. For years, our leaders had control over inflation and kept the interest rates historically low to stimulate our wounded economy.

With the war that Russia has declared on Ukraine and the response of the Western World, the gas price rose to the moon. That put even more pressure on inflation and for the last 4 months, inflation has spread like a stage 3 cancer.

To that our leaders had to react. They are responding with an increase in the interest rates to cold down the economy. They had no choice. But that's not only the economy that is slowing down but our hope and already very wounded morale.I am not playing the blame game here. For months, I asked the brightest finance and business people that I knew for ways to keep inflation under control. Everyone responded with the same answer, to increase the interest rates. Since the beginning of 2022, the interest rates in Canada went from 0.25% to 1.50% by July 2022. Tomorrow, it is expected to be raised to 2.5 %. That's basically 10 times the interest rates when we started the year.

Of course, that is hurting many people. The governments themselves are hurt since that will have to be taken care of in their budgets, now that they just took such big debts and deficits to face the Pandemic. So, let's make it crystal clear here, this is not about blaming anyone. We are all in this together, we are all in trouble! But again, I would like to raise my voice for the entrepreneurial class, too busy keeping our broken system afloat. As many if not all of them have taken a huge amount of loans to patch for the pandemic shortages, how would this increase in interest affect them?

Well, all will try to face the storm for as long as possible before being completely submerged under water. That is happening while the others are fighting for the system's survival with fewer and fewer hope and smaller and smaller buffer and range of movements. I raised that question to Quebec's Minister of Economy, Pierre Fitzgibbon in a private meeting. His answer was straight to the point and very honest. Entrepreneurs have to accept to be diluted. In other words, entrepreneurs have to appeal to governments and private investment funds to face the upcoming storm.

Well, for one, not all of our enterprises and companies will qualify for such investments. Facing an explosion in interest rates, entrepreneurs have barely kept their heads above water, but investment funds are now less and less favourable to invest in. That is not even counting the fact that the cost of money is now more expensive.

2.5% is not the highest interest rate ever but going 10 times the rates within 7 months, is pretty steep. And what will happen as the entrepreneurial class is falling, one after the next? Do you even know how long it would take to replace them? More than a generation! Those are the people who are paying to work! So yes, inflation must be dealt with. The shortage of staff has to be addressed faster and more aggressively than we had done. Our health professionals need reinforcement, empowerment, and gratification. That too has to take place as we speak. But we cannot do any of that while killing the hope of a return to normality and raising the smoke that a global recession is ahead.

Experts will debate on if the recession is coming or not and the opinions are all spread across the board. Those are what they are, opinions. Well, when there are so many expert opinions contradicting one another, the general opinion is to assume the worst. If the population is expecting the worst to come, they will act in such a way that all of the problems we described above will materialize at even a faster rate and will take biblical proportions. This is a demographic and social-economical phenomenon, made by people, and amplified by people. The only question is are we in control or are we simply reacting?

Do you remember what happened the last time that we faced an energy crisis that skyrocketed the interest rates? Interest rates went as up as 20% and plunged the world into a long recession. Well, that one did not have 30 months of pandemic wearing them down previously.

It is with that motivation and determination that I kept pushing the discussion and aligning bright minds to be creative and come up with solutions and alternatives. This is how André Châtelain, a mentor and friend, answered my call. Former first vice-president of the Mouvement Desjardins, André is bringing his experience and wisdom to the table. Joining are also Tranie Vo, COO of Mdex & Co., standing for the women entrepreneurs, and François Dufour, veteran vice-president of business development.

To make sure that our plans will also be answering the needs of our future, my son, William Bak, prodigy author and the youngest Alpha, has asked to have a seat at the table too. He asked, and who am I to say no?

Join us as we are sharing with you our findings and the solutions to avoid the dead-end crisis ahead. This is hope, we still have the time to act, and we have a plan. This is **COVIDCONOMICS, TAMING INFLATION WITHOUT INCREASING INTEREST RATES.**

Welcome to the Alphas.

> **I REFUSE TO BELIEVE THAT THE ONLY MEANS TO FIGHT INFLATION IS BY RAISING THE INTEREST RATES AND KILLING OUR ENTREPRENEURIAL CLASS IN THE PROCESS**
> Dr. Bak Nguyen

CHAPTER 1
"DIFFERENTIAL DIAGNOSTIC"
ANALYSIS OF THE CAUSES OF THE INFLATION CRISIS OF 2022

BY Dr. BAK NGUYEN & FRANÇOIS DUFOUR

"Not all inflations are the same."
Dr. Bak Nguyen

Allow me to borrow from my medical background to approach the problem. In medicine, there are symptoms and causes. As patients are complaining about the symptoms, which are signs and pains that they feel, that's not the actual illness to treat. As doctors, we are easing the symptoms but to treat, we need to address the illness itself. In other words, what caused the symptoms to start with?

One of the bases of medicine is to understand that many illnesses can have the same symptoms. Untreated symptoms will lead to complications. Solving the complications will be mandatory, but that is still not healing the illness itself, and either we will apply the wrong treatment and the symptoms will manifest again. So if I employ the same logic, is inflation a cancer (illness) as we called it? Is it a symptom or is it a complication? I am sure that different experts will have different opinions. That is why, I asked my co-author, François Dufour, an economist by trade, to give us his analysis.

In the meantime, here's my differential diagnosis. Inflation is a complication, happening because something else went wrong first. Just like the body, our economic system is an equilibrium, balancing and buffering many different demographic elements: supply, productivity, transport, distribution, wages, raw materials, demand…

All the elements are variable and always changing. Since the globalization of our supply chain, the system is forever changing and adapting. But we have made it so it can buffer much without bursting. Let's go through each of these elements and put them in the context of what led to the inflation crisis of 2022. SUPPLY: well, there was no significant shortage, as we started 2020, the world production was steady. Then COVID happened and countries all around the world shut down temporarily their production to limit the spread of the COVID virus.

For our lifetime, that was the first-ever shutdown of the complete chain of productivity, from RAW MATERIAL to PRODUCTIVITY to DISTRIBUTION. We all did that internationally and around the same time. As a consequence, our system had simply very little buffers, and everything shut down. But different countries have different policies and different waves of infection. Once we started shutting down the world's productivity, it took a while to see its effect. We still had reserves and our buffers helped stabilize the situation.

I don't know if you remembered, but at the beginning of the pandemic, our leaders were talking about shutting down for 2 weeks! Well, we all know too well what happened after. No blame here, nobody really knew what was really going on. For months and months, we were in reaction mode.

What is really a reaction mode? Well, it is to look at the signs and symptoms and make our decisions accordingly. The irony of this inflation is that it is literally the complication of a virus, COVID. So as COVID spread around the world, different countries shut down at different moments, but all doing basically the same thing. If you look at the historical data, it was pretty similar to the different time zones following the rotation of the Earth.

As soon as possible, different countries resumed their production as their experts were evaluating the COVID viral risks. On and off, we slowed, stalled, and even stopped the world's SUPPLY chain. So if we've started by taking a *"PAUSE"*, the pauses were different in every single region of the planet. At first, that was more of a symphony as all the world leaders were reacting, more or less in unison. But that *"GLOBAL PAUSE"* has never fully resumed, since different countries had different timings, all reacting to COVID. As a result, the whole system is in buffering mode ever since.

It took a few months, but the supply chain started showing weaknesses and voids in 2020. The shortage of chips affecting the car industry is a great example. Since most of the world's automobile makers were having their parts from the global economy, they were all missing the same chip. As a result, a huge halt happened worldwide that could not be foreseen by a single organization, no matter the brand.

As a consequence, there was a shortage in new car deliveries. Car Dealerships ran out of stock and the price of the secondary car market saw a huge increase in value. Yes, used cars were gaining in value since they are now hot commodities! That's just an example.

Different countries had different timing, but basically, all reacted in the same way. Let's put that in the context of the globalization in which we operate. Some countries are RAW MATERIAL producers. Some countries are more dedicated to the TRANSFORMATION of raw materials into products. Some others excel in TRANSPORT. Only our DISTRIBUTION systems are regional. But our response, internationally, was the same. Eventually, our population was put in pause, stopping or at least decreasing its productivity outcome. Because of the difference in timing and the spreading of that reaction over the last 30 months, well, our system in pause never fully resumed.

And by WE ARE ALL DOING THE SAME, what did we all do? Asking for people to stay home until ordered otherwise. No matter in which industry you were from, no matter from which country, during the last 30 months, the odds are pretty high that you have not produced as much as before. That was often out of your control.

Well, putting people on pause for more than 2 weeks, then readjusting, and asking them to work remotely started another phenomenon: the EXODUS. In Asia, stories of people exiting the cities to go back to their hometowns and villages are not common but a standard. There were ever horror stories about families stuck between borders as the different local authorities shut down their local frontier.

In the west, people were moving out of the city. Once the schools were shut down, nothing anchored most families anymore. Those who had the means migrated from their condo into bigger homes in the suburbs and even beyond. Megacities like New York were emptying up. If you need concrete proof, look at the real estate market of New York City for the last 30 months and the numbers talk for themselves. In 2022, if you visit New York City, you will see how few construction cranes are in the city. 5 years ago, anywhere you turned your eyes, you could see construction cranes.

Not all the people moved, only those who could afford to do so did. That changed the topography of the demographic. As schools resumed with homeschooling, families had the time to move and readjust to their new environment. That's only a part of the story. More people were asking to take a forced leave from work, waiting for demand to resume. These 2 weeks became months and years. They too had to readjust and many, tired of waiting, changed industries, jobs or, simply just left.

Others had much time on their hands to rethink their life choices and career.

Since it is commonly known that most people work for a living, now that work was gone or on pause, living took more and more importance.

Dr. Bak Nguyen

It was like everyone was going through an existential crisis or a midlife crisis at the same time. Well, what is unique here is that happened all at once, internationally.

Some other people got pregnant, twice within the last 30 months, leading to many maternity leaves! That too, changed the demographic and the active population at work. Also, the more experienced workforce who were thinking of retiring eventually, COVID gave them the push they needed to move on and not turn back. Stack together all of these demographic phenomena and you have the shortage of staff that the world started to experience by 2021.

Consequently, as the economy resumed, production decreased and even stalled in some sectors. Wages exploded and suddenly, the structure of society was turned upside down: employers are now begging their employees to work. It results not only in wages increase but also in working conditions and business hours too! That, each industry has its own story to tell.

The most recent example I can give you to illustrate how our system has never fully unpaused is the actual crisis in our airports as citizens are finally allowed to travel internationally after more than 2 years. Even if the borders were not closed for the whole 30 months, it took close to 24 months before the vaccination of the whole family could be completed. By summer 2022, as soon as the school year ended, fully vaccinated families looking for these long-awaited vacations, flooded the airports.

Airport crews were not fully staffed, due to the market conditions and restrictions of the last 30 months. Facing the demand, employers called back their workforce on forced leave. Well, what do you know? They left, changed industries, moved away, etc.

That is how, in 2022, the news are talking about the delays in airports and the nightmare in luggage logistics, at least in Canada. No blame, just facts. So is the shortage of staff a problem? Of course! But that's a symptom of a much bigger demographic phenomenon.

So, shortage of staff, an explosion in wages, shortage of stock, and even disruption in the transport of goods, all contributed to the increase of inflation. And since the Beijing Olympic Games, China has reported an alarming increase in COVID spread. As a result, their authorities shut down entire cities, one after the next. China being the manufactory of the world, how do you think that it will affect the global system?

So all of these factors led to an increase in inflation, because production sunk when demand remained pretty much the same.

All of these are major demographic phenomena that caused the explosion of inflation, right?

Let's look at some numbers on inflation for North America and Europe widely available on a simple Google search.

INFLATION

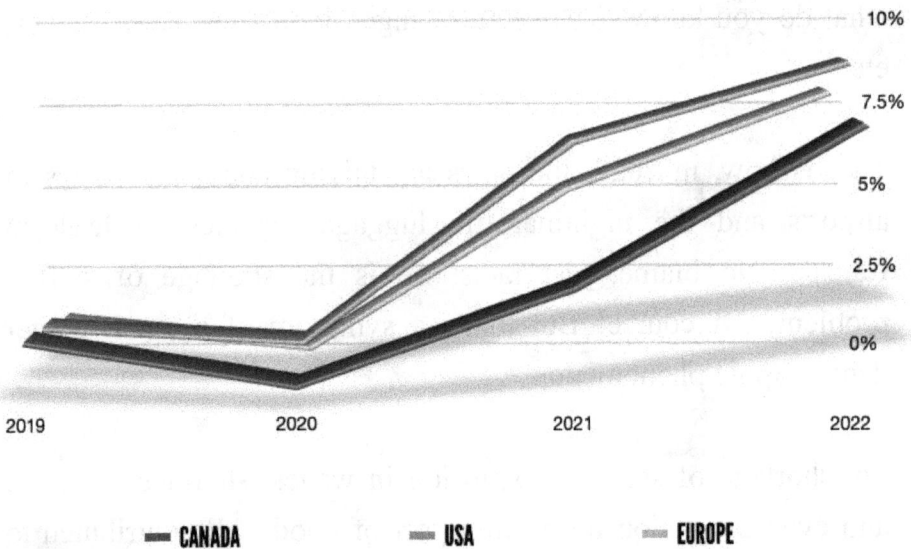

2022	CANADA	ÉTATS-UNIS	EUROPE
Jan	5,1%	7,5%	5,6%
Fev	5,7%	7,9%	6,2%
Mars	6,7%	8,5%	7,8%
Avril	6,8%	8,3%	8,1%
Mai	7,7%	8,6%	8,8%
Juin		9,1%	

Looking at the number, we can all see how inflation has evolved within the last 30 months. By 2020, inflation decreased all across the board, even if production sank. That can be explained by a decrease in demand due to COVID and the reserve the global system had as a buffer.

By 2021, the shortage of staff and the manifestation of the different demographic phenomena taking place affected the inflation rate. But by 2022, what happened?

INFLATION

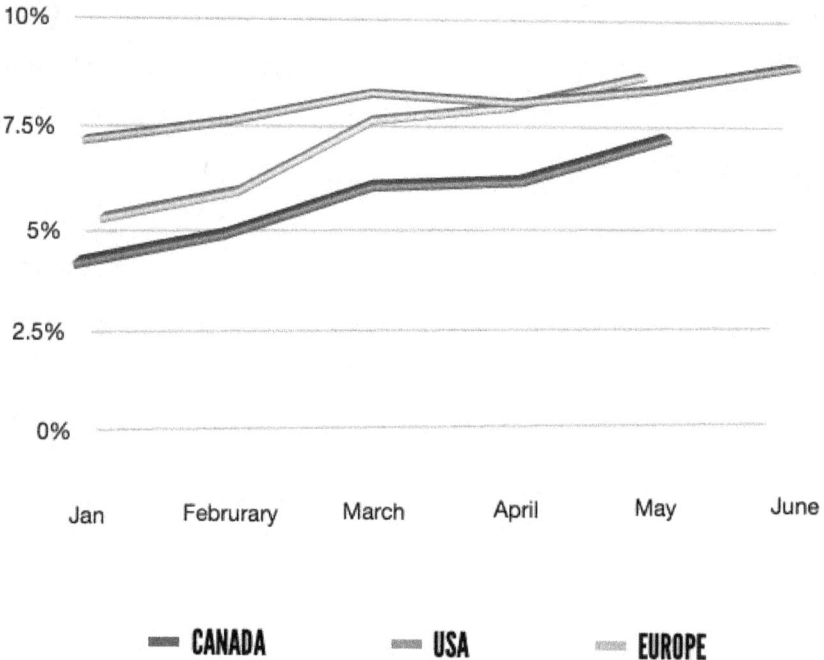

CANADA   USA   EUROPE

2022	CANADA	ÉTATS-UNIS	EUROPE
2019	1,95%	1,81%	1,44%
2020	0,72	1,4%	0,68%
2021	3,4%	7%	5,35
2022	7,7% (MAI)	9,1% (JUIN)	8,1% (MAI)

Please note that the worst inflation rate (by MAY 2022) in Europe were Estonia (20.1%), Lithuania (18.5%), and Latvia (16.8%). These 3 countries had very different inflation rates by May 2021: Estonia (3.2%), Lithuania (3.5%), and Latvia (2.6%).

By May 2021, the world was already in pandemic for more than a year, and inflation was, somehow, raising but under control. Then, we ran out of buffers. But what really happened in 2022? How did we go from 3.4% to 7% in Canada between 2021 and June 2022? How the USA went from 7% to 9% and Europe, going from 5.35% to 8.1% during the same period?

Except for the USA, the trend is very clear for Canada and Europe which saw a huge increase by 2022. What happened? This is what I meant by differential. Before jumping to any conclusion, I will let my friend and colleague, François Dufour, economist, to present to you his analysis and explanations.

HYPERINFLATION

The Second World War was partly triggered by hyperinflation. The German population needed a wheelbarrow of cash to buy a simple loaf of bread. That hyperinflation brought a great deal of poverty and despair which lead to political turmoil, the rise of fascism, and the horrors that the world witnessed.

We are far from this reality, but we must always remember this tragic part of human History. Right now, the CPI growth in the United States is 9.1% year over year versus 2.0% in April 2019. That drastic increase reminds me of a famous quote

"Compound interest is the eighth wonder of the world. He who understands it, earns it. He who doesn't, pays it."

Albert Einstein

Germany's 1920s Inflation

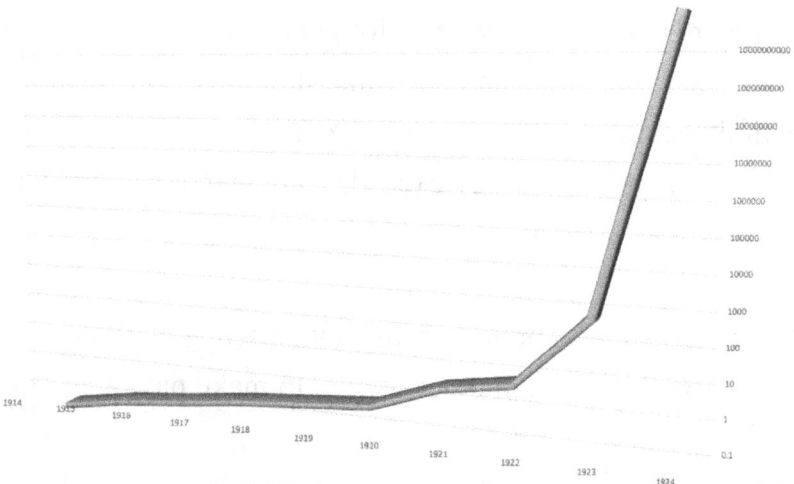

In other words, we may be facing a force that is extremely difficult to control. The above graphic of Germany's inflation in the 20s shows a clear danger ahead.

We can see on that graph a clear exponential formula that creeps in the first few years to finally explode in that typical hockey stick figure (being Canadian, it is mandatory to use this analogy). One of the reasons for this dramatic event is the impact of World War 1 spending. Germany did witness a very costly and prolonged war at the beginning of the century. Wars are the main reason for spending and inflation.

What exactly causes this force to strive an increase at an exponential rate? Simply put, SUPPLY and DEMAND. Everybody knows that when the supply of a good exceeds the demand, it makes the good, per se less desirable, or in economic terms, gives it a reduced utility.

A typical good could be the supply of cars, if the market is flooded with cars and it far exceeds the demand for them, we can expect a decrease in the prices of cars. The same can be applied to money, when governments spend money (prints money in other words) to make payments for good and services, an external force with its rules of its own come into play. The spending has no limit hence the flooding of the market with actual money. When the supply of money exceeds its demand, we can witness a decrease in its value/utility.

The same can be applied to money, when governments spend money (prints money in other words) to make payments for good and services, an external force with its rules of its own come into play. The spending has no limit hence the flooding of the market with actual money. When the supply of money exceeds its demand, we can witness a decrease in its value/utility.

Let's explore a few economic policies that happened recently that increased inflationary pressures on the currency. We will look at the issue from a US perspective to give the reader a familiar frame of reference.

THE CLINTON HOMEOWNERSHIP COMMUNITY REINVESTMENT ACT

Community Reinvestment Act regulators gave banks higher ratings for home loans made in 'credit-deprived' areas. Furthermore, credit scores and income stability were no longer a criterion for borrowing money at such institutions as Freddie Mac and Fanny Mae (the two federally backed home mortgage companies).

That increased access to home ownership and pushed the prices of real estate upward, hence creating more money on the market. When Grandpa would sell his house paid at $40,000 for $1 million, we would witness a massive amount of money going into the economy. Grandpa would then turn around and buy consumer goods, thus increasing the prices of all goods as demand increased faster than supply, not only for the good in question but also for an inverse correlation to the value of money.

Some would also argue that the Community Reinvestment Act is one of the causes of the subprime crisis in 2008 that led to a recession that we will discuss later in this chapter.

The war in Iraq and Afghanistan

These wars were probably the single biggest expenditures in the history of mankind. 8 trillion dollars is the latest figure. Indeed, not only the cost of weapons, personnel, equipment, and logistics but also the aftershock of the wars such as veteran costs.

Not to forget the social issues stem from wars, such as the loss of a family member. Those social issues end up bearing a heavy cost to society. The campaigns of Iraq and Afghanistan, per se, cost around 6 trillion dollars in total costs but cost another 2 trillion dollars for veterans until 2050 (Watson Institute of Brown University's formula). That influx of money in the American economy is equivalent to 5 times the annual GDP of Canada. An enormous sum of money of undeniable proportions that increases the supply of money.

THE SUBPRIME CRISIS

In 2008, the subprime crisis that led to a global recession created some of the most shocking bankruptcies in the history of capitalism. To name a few: Lehman Brothers, CIT Group, Chrysler, GM, Ambac, Guaranty Financial Corp, Tribune Company, and Charter Communications.

Some of those companies have completely disappeared from the map. As you were reading the list you probably realized that some of those companies still exist, and some are very much thriving, thanks to the US government BAILOUT.

The costs of these bailouts amounted to $498 billion according to the MIT. Another act of printing money as one would say. The term printing money is often used in day-to-day life when talking about government spending since the FED got off the Gold Standards in 1971 under Richard Nixon's presidency, which pegged every dollar on the gold in reserve, when $35 equated to one ounce of gold. Before 1971, every dollar that was in your wallet could be technically exchanged for gold. This was giving money a value, a utility but also controlling its supply as gold is a mineral with limited supply.

Following President Nixon's act, the expression PRINTING MONEY is now referred to as the phenomenon of the US federal government has no holds barred when it's time to spend. With executive orders or with passed bills, the government can increase its spending at will without any constraint of a limited supply of money. The government has access to an inexhaustible well of capital that will never dry out. Once again, increasing the money supply available on the market.

THE COVID-19 PANDEMIC

Another event that was certainly not planned nor predicted was the global pandemic of Covid-19. The pandemic put the economy on pause for a couple of years. Some might say that the timing was perfect to slow down the already overheated economy at full employment. But the pandemic had much most severe repercussions on the day-to-day. Repercussions that were not anticipated and could not even be imagined. Again, the government had to dispense a lot of money into the economy to help with businesses, people's income supplement, sanitary measures, equipment, and logistics for the healthcare sector.

Also, expenditures were made on the scientific research for a vaccine and then once in production, the purchase of millions of doses of the vaccine. The USA spent about $4.5 trillion on the Covid relief programs and Canada, which is 10 times less populated, spent about $600 billion.The money supply increased to the same tune in the economy, a major inflationary pressure upward but some other economic factors were not taken into consideration for the recovery time.

In fact, supply chains were impacted putting another form of pressure on the prices, the supply of goods is impacted but contrary to the supply of money, the supply of goods has been impacted negatively. A reduction in supply will result in higher prices if the demand stays the same.

The supply chains have been impacted for the following reasons: a lot of factories had to close under the covid mandate to reduce the spread of the virus but also a lot of people decided to retire given the situation in place. If they were hesitating before Covid, that was the little nudge that made them make up their minds.

Given also that the western world has an aging population, we saw a disproportionate number of people going into retirement. That shortage of labour/workers had a direct impact on production and supply chains.

THE UKRAINE INVASION

Another major event going on at the time of writing this book is the invasion of Ukraine by Russia. The US government has spent about $56 billion in military aid so far, another influx of capital and devaluation of money given the increased supply. The conflict not only increased government spending but also instigated a traders' frenzy as the price of the barrel of oil increased by multiples folds. The economic sanctions on Russia created a short supply on the global market.

It is well stated in this book that this price increase has significantly impacted the prices of all goods and commodities as their transport is now 2 to 3 times more expensive. This severe shock to the supply of oil and its severe price increase at the gas pump triggered Dr. Bak's initiative to write this book. We are discussing a solution to go over the control of the price of oil.

Nowadays, given that we are no longer using the gold standard, and we are in currency free for all, there are a few mechanisms that can be utilized to control the supply of money. As per Milton Friedman, the number one tool would be to increase the interest rates. There are 2 ways to do so: the overnight bank rate set by the government but also the issuing of debt.

In fact, by issuing debt, it can work in 2 ways. First, by removing circulating currencies as people will decrease borrowing. Secondly, the increase in interest will make saving more attractive, therefore, once again, helping to reduce the money in circulation.

Another way is to control the cost of labour which has been done in the early 80s and ended up as a total fiasco as the prices could not adjust quickly enough to maintain the purchasing power of the workers. Another way is to control and the price of energy, therefore reducing the costs of goods across the board through the whole supply chain.

Join us as we are sharing with you our findings and a solution to avoid the dead-end crisis ahead. This is hope, we still have the time to act, and we have a plan. This is **COVIDCONOMICS, TAMING INFLATION WITHOUT INCREASING INTEREST RATES.**

Welcome to the Alphas.

I REFUSE TO BELIEVE THAT THE ONLY MEANS
TO FIGHT INFLATION IS BY RAISING THE INTEREST RATES
AND KILLING OUR ENTREPRENEURIAL CLASS IN THE PROCESS
Dr. Bak Nguyen[1]

1 https://www.businessinsider.com/weimar-germany-hyperinflation-explained-2013-9
2 https://watson.brown.edu/costsofwar/
3 https://mitsloan.mit.edu/ideas-made-to-matter/heres-how-much-2008-bailouts-really-cost
4 https://www.usaspending.gov/disaster/covid-19?publicLaw=all
5 https://nationalpost.com/news/politics/federal-government-has-spent-576b-in-new-measures-since-start-of-covid-pandemic-pbo-report

CHAPTER 2
"THE PERFECT STORM"

BY Dr. BAK NGUYEN

Even if we often say that History repeats itself, it is not always 100% true. Each crisis is particular with its own specifications. We've just covered the 2022 inflation crisis and what led to its burst.

> **"If fire needs air to breathe and oil to burst, inflation feeds on fear and oil."**
>
> Dr. Bak Nguyen

Fear and the lack of oil are mainly what caused inflation to rise vertically. In Canada, war and the price of oil pushed the inflation rate from 3.4% to 7.7% by May 2022; in Europe, that went from 5.35% to 8.1% during the same period. In the USA, inflation jumped from 7% (2021) to 9.1% by June 2022. Well, the pandemic and its effect caused the first set of numbers until 2022. That's inflation, but one due to the Pandemic and the shortages following.

What happened by the end of February 2022 was the beginning of the invasion of Ukraine by Russia. After international condemnation, the Western world took severe economical measures to react to the declaration of war by Russia.

What was an invasion on a military front of a superpower invading a neighbour country became an economical war between Russia and the Western world. Measures announced took weeks and months to take effect, and yet, inflation started spiking right away. Here is a map of Europe and the inflation rates comparing May 2022 and May 2021, and its geo-localization from the proximity to the war zone (Ukraine).

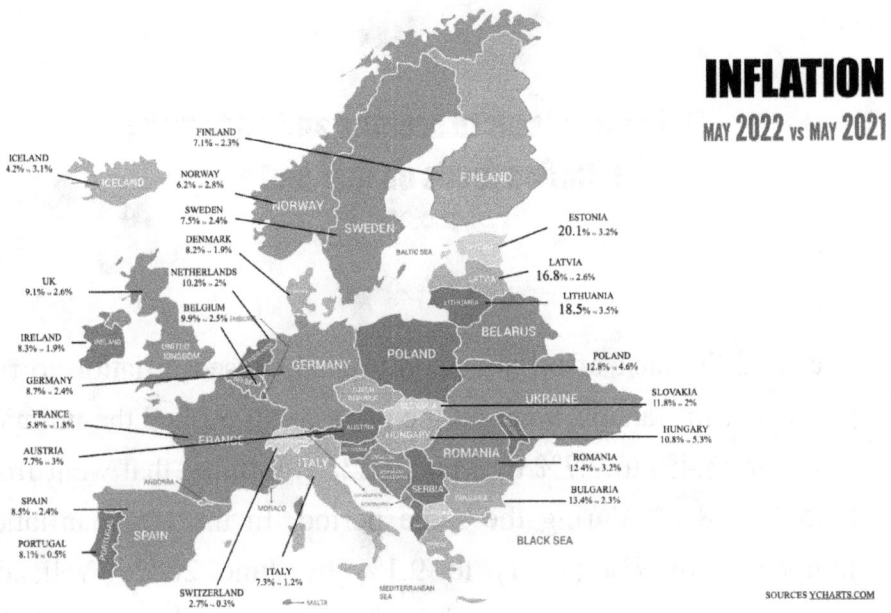

INFLATION

MAY 2022 vs MAY 2021

ICELAND
4.2% - 3.1%

FINLAND
7.1% - 2.3%

NORWAY
6.2% - 2.8%

SWEDEN
7.5% - 2.4%

DENMARK
8.2% - 1.9%

ESTONIA
20.1% - 3.2%

LATVIA
16.8% - 2.6%

NETHERLANDS
10.2% - 2%

LITHUANIA
18.5% - 3.5%

UK
9.1% - 2.6%

BELGIUM
9.9% - 2.5%

IRELAND
8.3% - 1.9%

POLAND
12.8% - 4.6%

GERMANY
8.7% - 2.4%

SLOVAKIA
11.8% - 2%

FRANCE
5.8% - 1.8%

HUNGARY
10.8% - 5.3%

AUSTRIA
7.7% - 3%

ROMANIA
12.4% - 3.2%

SPAIN
8.5% - 2.4%

BULGARIA
13.4% - 2.3%

PORTUGAL
8.1% - 0.5%

BLACK SEA

ITALY
7.3% - 1.2%

SWITZERLAND
2.7% - 0.3%

SOURCES YCHARTS.COM

40

As you can see, inflation exploded across the board in 2022, while in 2021, after more than 12 months of pandemic, inflation remained "under control". The other interesting fact that I would like to point out is how high the inflation rates of these countries closest to Russia are, as they are fearing the same fate as Ukraine (invasion).

The **FEAR FACTOR** is undeniable. Estonia, Latvia, and Lithuania are now showing an inflation rate that is more than double the average of the European continent. Before the war, their inflation rate was well within the average of Europe.

So how the **FEAR FACTOR** affects inflation? Well, inflation is the result of the balance between demand and offer. With fear in place, either demand spiked due to behaviour changes, either productivity tanked also due to behaviour changes or, what is more plausible would be the combination of both.

There were no specific embargos targeting these countries between May 2021 and May 2022. That emphasizes the impact of the domestic behaviour factor (FEAR) on the rates of inflation. Moving away from Ukraine, the inflation rate decreased. That is to illustrate the isolated effect of the WAR and the **FEAR FACTOR**.

"Inflation is a crowd phenomenon."
Dr. Bak Nguyen

Caught in a stampede, if you want to survive, you have to run in the same direction, as fast as possible not to be stamped on. Eventually, you may have to outrun the crowd, even if you never really understood why you were running in the first place.

And that is the effect of the Ukraine invasion on the rate of inflation, it started with fear and people reacted proportional to their proximity to the zone of conflict. The more secure they feel, the least they react. But as soon as the population feels the heat, they are amplifying the stampede tenfold and even more.

So what do you think happened as the interest rate keep increasing to send the signal that we should cold down the economy? With a 1% increase by the Central Bank of Canada in July 2022, what signal are we sending to the population, one far from the Russian borders? We are spreading fear! Is that the right cure? I know, our economists are not to blame, they only have one single weapon to fight inflation and it is by raising the interest rate.

"It is time for us to ask more questions and to be more creative, and consequential."

Dr. Bak Nguyen

In the last chapter, I was wondering why is it that, in the USA, inflation jumped differently, from 7% by the end of 2021 to 9.1% by June 2022? I made some research in that sense. Do you know that the USA has a **STRATEGIC PETROLEUM RESERVE (SPR)** of 727 million barrels of crude?

Even if inflation rates were high in 2021, as the Biden administration took economical sanctions against Russia and planned to band their oil from the world market, they buffered part of that effect thanks to their own oil reserves. By July 2022, the gas price at the pump decreased in most of North America due to the release announced by the Biden administration to sell crude to Europe and Asia. That is a million barrels of crude released per day over the next 6 months, in the effort to curb gas prices. That's the biggest withdrawal from the SPR in History.

Even if inflation is not solely due to gas prices, alone, gas prices are dictating the rate of inflation. The last decision of the USA illustrates that importance. So don't be mistaken, we are at war. But who are we fighting? Russia? I will let you draw your own conclusion. But if we go back in History, here's what happened the last time that we had an energy crisis of this amplitude.

In October 1973, the Organization of Arab Petroleum Countries led by Saudi Arabia led an oil embargo against the USA, United Kingdom, Canada, Japan, the Netherlands, Portugal, Rhodesia, and South Africa. The price of the crude barrel went up 300%, from $3 to $12 by the end of 1974. This hit hard as the USA were declining their domestic Oil production since 1959.

That started a long economical war with devastating effects on the world economy. The embargo was lifted in March 1974 but affected the value of the US dollar, weakening its position in the world market through the rest of the 1970s.

Consequently, inflation rose in the double digits. By the early 80s, the Federal Reserve increased interest rates to react to fight inflation. That spike in inflation was due to oil prices combined with a weak dollar. During the following years, 1981 and 1982, the USA would see little or no economical growth as interest rates kept rising. Unemployment rose from 3.8% to 24% from 1978 to 1982.

What started in 1973 as an energy crisis set the stage for 3 recessions, 1973-75, 1980-82, and 1990-91. If the price of oil started the cascade to burst inflation, interest rates were responsible for the next 2 recessions, consecutively.

If we put all of this in perspective, the price of oil started a chain reaction leading to inflation. That oil war lasted from 1973-74, but inflation kept rising. As a reaction, central banks raised their interest rates, causing the 2 following recessions, over the next 16 years. This is just to illustrate how the oil price is key to inflation and how our remedy to inflation will have long terms scars on our economy and societies. Not just because the price of borrowing is higher, but because of the signal it sends, insecurity and fear!

"Inflation is a crowd phenomenon."

Dr. Bak Nguyen

Put that in perspective of this crisis, fear and division already got the best of us over the last 30 months. In other words, the fire is well installed. Now, add to that the oil factor, and inflation is out of control. To inflation, our response is to increase the interest rates, in other words, to bring the message of fear inside of our borders. That will be felt on a daily basis. What do you think will happen next?

That's not all, the first collateral damage of increasing interest rates as we discussed in the introduction will be to kill all of our entrepreneurial class. Who will lead the economic come back? The crisis that started in 1973-74 was not as systemic and globalization was not as extensive as today. This is the perfect storm raising, and even if we are only reacting, the most damaging effect is the remedy we are adopting to fight the fever (inflation).

3 recessions over the course of 16 years affected an economical war based on oil prices. Are we prepared to face such consequences yet again? Excuse me, this crisis will be much broader and will hit much harder if the actual trends keep their course.

"The Inflation crisis of 2022 is growing into the perfect storm."
Dr. Bak Nguyen

My place is not to label or to tell you what to think, I just want you to have the information and to make your own opinion on the seriousness of this present crisis.

Inflation is spiking, but what is its real cause? And on which factors can we address the issue? Numbers are showing how influential the oil crude price is over inflation. The comparison of the numbers between May 2021 and May 2022 clearly isolates the **OIL FACTOR**.

Then, with the geography of Europe, the numbers also clearly illustrate how the **FEAR FACTOR** contributes to burst inflation into orbit. Is our remedy taming those or it is feeding them? And before we conclude this chapter, there is still one phenomenon that I would like to come back to: the inflation rate of 2020.

INFLATION

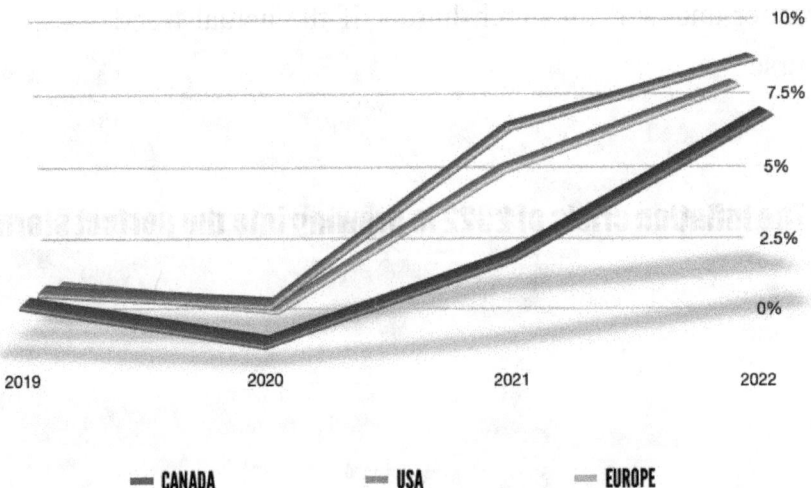

2019	2020	2021	2022

— CANADA　　　— USA　　　— EUROPE

How can we explain that inflation decreased in 2020 when the whole world was in the initial pause of more or less 3 months in reaction to the pandemic declared by the World Health Organization (WHO)?

If you look at the graphic, you can clearly see a dip in inflation in 2020. Inflation is due when demand exceeds the offer. In 2020, the offering stall, for at least 3 months! As mentioned earlier, our global system had buffers. But was that enough to justify the reverse inflation?

Think of it really hard, when the pandemic was declared, where were you? What were you doing? How did you feel? You were surely in shock, in disbelief, and wondering when you would wake up from this weird dream. Then the weird ran as a loop, for days, weeks, and months.

What you saw and missed was also the price of gas at the pump. Immediately after the official announcement of a pandemic, gas prices tanked and remained low for the rest of 2020. While the average price of the crude barrel was $64.30 in 2019, it went down to average $41.96 in 2020 with the lowest tag price of $12.78. Then it went back up to average $70.68 in 2021. By 2022, the average price for the first 6 months is $106.92.

CRUDE BARREL PRICE

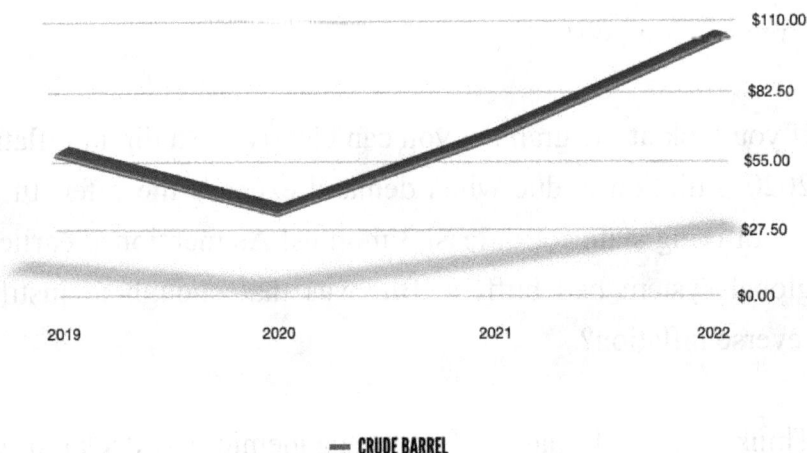

Can you see the resemblance of that curve with the Canadian inflation rate curve for the same years? It is practically a copy-paste.

I would like to underline that the spirit of this work is not to point fingers but to clearly see and understand what happened, beyond the headlines, the rumours, and the daily media. We need to understand to not feed the frenzy and the trends that would just make matters worse.

Join us as we are sharing with you our findings and a solution to avoid the dead-end crisis ahead. This is hope, we still have the time to act, and we have a plan. This is **COVIDCONOMICS, TAMING INFLATION WITHOUT INCREASING INTEREST RATES.**

Welcome to the Alphas.

I REFUSE TO BELIEVE THAT THE ONLY MEANS
TO FIGHT INFLATION IS BY RAISING THE INTEREST RATES
AND KILLING OUR ENTREPRENEURIAL CLASS IN THE PROCESS
Dr. Bak Nguyen

CHAPTER 3
"FREE MARKET COSTS"

THE SPOILS AND CASUALTIES OF WARS

BY ANDRÉ CHÂTELAIN & Dr. BAK NGUYEN

We live in a capitalist and free market world. The ups and downs of the price of goods and services are part of that system. The value of our money will also influence our buying power. A weak currency will even fuel recessions like the one of 1980-82. So monetary policy is of prime importance.

What did our governments do during the last 30 months to fight COVID, to protect their population, to finance vaccination efforts and to keep the economy from free falling? Well, it printed and borrowed money in the trillions. According to normal math, that is weakening its currency. But since most governments around the world all did the same thing at the same time, we did not see a burst, just an increase of some points in inflation in 2021. For reference, the USA printed 6.5 trillion for 2020 and 2021.

Canada has a different monetary system, one in which it cannot simply print money and spend it. The Canadian federal source of income are taxes, duties, interest, and penalties collected. If the Canadian federal government spends more than its income, it creates a deficit that it will have to borrow to cover. For reference, the Canadian Federal debt added $344 billion for the exercise of 2020-21 and $95.6 billion for the fiscal year of 2021-22.

In a word, both the Federal governments of North America had a monetary policy that usually depreciates their money. But it was in reaction to an unprecedented crisis, one in which most, if not all the governments of the world did the same, at different proportions. Keep in mind that the deep recession of 1980-82 was due to inflation deriving from a weak dollar.

The recession of 1990-91 was caused by high-interest rates. What are we doing now as our national debts are through the roof, with a lost currency value combined with the increase of interest rate and crazy high crude price? That is really what we called the perfect storm, reproducing the conditions of the recession of 1973-74, 1980-82, and 1990-91 all combined! It's like the ALL STARS of Inflation and Recession. That is, on top of COVID!

At least, we all should know in what direction our collective destiny is heading! By the end of the first chapter, we also saw the similitude in crude price and inflation, as in Canada, it almost mirrored one another. So let's cover petroleum and the energy sector more in-depth, shall we?

The international market of petroleum is a free market. Is that market really free? We all heard the saying that nothing is really free. Influence, agenda, and geo-politico wars, all affect directly the free market of international goods and commodities. The truth is petroleum is a market greatly under the influence, almost a monopoly-like influence by a group named OPEC, (Organization of the Petroleum Exporting Countries) which includes 13 countries members with the control of 44% of the world oil production and own 81.5% of the world proven oil reserves. The OPEC controls directly the world supply of oil at any given time, therefore, the price of the crude barrel.

As the Ukraine invasion clearly illustrated, what happened on another continent will have direct consequences with its ripple effects. In the same line of thought, confinements of entire cities in China are having a direct effect on our supply chain and economy. The "not my problem" philosophy is now obsolete. And yet, there are so many factors out of our control.

We live in democratic countries. We vote to elect those in power who are making the decision for the greater good, for our good. Well, did you vote for the gas price? Do you have any influence on how China is governing its people?

Now you have a better understanding of globalization, monetary policies, inflation, and interest rates. And within this journey, you also clearly saw the direct correlation between gas price and inflation. Well, bright minds before us saw that too! In the USA, Presidents from both parties pushed to increase domestic production of energy and to diminish the dependency of the USA on external oil.

The advancement in technology on shale gas extraction combined with the tax incentives for unconventional gas harvesting created a new hope, one of energy independence.

From 2000 to 2014, both in the USA and in Canada, we saw the emergence of a new class of oil producers. Within the years 2010-13, the price of a crude barrel was averaging $100. To break even, shale gas extraction has to sell their barrel at $50 to $60, shale gas extraction being a process much more expensive than conventional oil drilling.

During that new era of energy, the USA's domestic production of gas was as high as 11 million barrels per day, the highest level since 1970. That translated into a significant drop in the dependence on external gas, from 60% in 2005 to 30% in 2016. Well, OPEC (Organization of the Petroleum Exporting Countries) did not like the idea of losing market shares and went into an offensive to kill the competition. It lowered the price of the crude barrel from above $110 to $46 and kept the price of crude below the $100 mark until February 2022. Between 2014 and 2022, the crude price fluctuated mainly between $40 and $60. In January 2016, the price of crude was at $30.

The OPEC's offensive of the last 8 years put much of the new entrepreneurial class in unconventional gas harvesting out of business.

"The first rule of a free market is that the lowest price is king."

Dr. Bak Nguyen

Now that crude prices are back above the $100 mark, it would have been a fair competition between shale gas and convention oil drilling, but most of the unconventional oil producers went out of business, leaving OPEC back in the monopoly seat.

Don't blame OPEC, they felt the menace and acted in such a way to protect their own interest. If there is any blame to assign, we should blame ourselves, always going for what is cheaper without a horizon of what will be following next. OPEC put out an offensive and we all drank its *coolaid* with a much lower gas price at the pump.

That "saving" profited the sectors and the companies heavy on energy as agriculture and transport. That saving was not always reflected in the tag price to the customers.

At the same time, OPEC countries accumulated deficits resulting in their own offensive of lowering the crude price. In 2015, Saudi Arabia accumulated 98 billion in deficit (21% of its GDP). Countries with less latitude like Venezuela fell into an economic depression. So the people did not always benefit from the low crude price.

In our economic model and western philosophy, a free market is our way of life. That's how it should be, but when the market is under a strong monopolistic influence, can we afford to play by the rule of the market when it is dictating so heavily our societies and living standards? The cost of energy is what fuel our economy, inflation, consumption, habits, and, when it comes to it, hard choices. This has to be fair!

We need to ask ourselves, as citizens of a society, is the fluctuation of the free market always a good thing for the evolution of our societies? Of course, we want freedom and freedom has its price. But is the freedom to pay higher, to work more, for the same good or service worth the fame and the fight?

We, my co-authors and myself, strongly believe that a certain stability is needed in our free market, especially on elements that affect our buying power and our lives as deeply as the cost of energy.

"Is the price of energy a major component in the right to dignity?"

Dr. Bak Nguyen

Join us as we are sharing with you our findings and a solution to avoid the dead-end crisis ahead. This is hope, we still have the time to act, and we have a plan. This is **COVIDCONOMICS, TAMING INFLATION WITHOUT INCREASING INTEREST RATES.**

Welcome to the Alphas.

I REFUSE TO BELIEVE THAT THE ONLY MEANS
TO FIGHT INFLATION IS BY RAISING THE INTEREST RATES
AND KILLING OUR ENTREPRENEURIAL CLASS IN THE PROCESS
Dr. Bak Nguyen

CHAPTER 4
"THE BUFFER MODEL"

FOR PEACE, STABILITY, AND PROSPERITY

BY ANDRÉ CHÂTELAIN & Dr. BAK NGUYEN

Inflation, inflation, inflation. What is acceptable? Well, an inflation rate below 3% will allow the growth of the country, protect the buying power and protect the standard of living of its citizens. Above 3%, things are spiralling toward heavy consequences.

With today's inflation at 8.1% in Canada and 9.1% in the USA by June 2022, inflation is not only high but what is alarming is how quickly it rose. By the end of 2021, Canada was at 3.4% and the USA at 7%. So as cautious as we want to be, it is spiralling out of control!

That's also why the Canadian Central Bank increased by tenfold, literally, its interest rate in 2021, from 0.25% to 2.5% by mid-July 2022. The key factor is the price of energy, the price of crude, rising from $68 by the end of December 2021 to $104 by July 2022. By the time of this writing, the crude barrel is tagged at $96.50, after the decision of the Biden administration to release 1 million barrels per day from the Strategic Petroleum Reserve (SPR).

So if inflation was climbing from the different factors post-pandemic, crude price by itself caused the spiral and inflation storm now on everyone's mind. And that's the free market!

"There is nothing free about this market, especially when people don't even have a real choice."

Dr. Bak Nguyen

And the free market is not solely to be blamed, we are now living the consequences of the globalization we chose to embrace. There are pros and cons, as the perfect solution does not exist. But we strongly believe that the basis vectors of our economy and standard of life as the cost of energy should be standardized and stabilized.

But before blaming OPEC, let's, once again, study the numbers of the past and their impact on our historical data. By the second half of 2013, crude barrel price was already above $100. And yet, inflation was nowhere near where it is now. The gas price at the pump averaged $3.62 the gallon in the USA. By June 2022, as the crude barrel was averaging $120, the gas price at the pump was hitting $5 the gallon!

In Canada, the gas price pump was averaging $1.28 per litre by 2013 and $2.11 by June 2022. Can you see a disproportion in the tag price to the consumers, in other words, to the society as a whole, for the same exact product, one essential to the function of our economy, supply and production chain? This isn't a free market, but not at all!

How much longer will we accept this hostage situation blaming the wrong actors? Go through the historical data and the trend is clear. A few are holding the keys to our society and standard of living, dictating almost directly, the inflation rates.

As we have clearly illustrated, the increase of interest rates, at this pace, will fuel the **FEAR factor**, leading to even more inflation and spiralling our economy and society into a path to the biggest economic recession so far, combining all the major components of the recessions of 1972-73, 1980-82, and 1990-91. Post-pandemic, that also means killing our entrepreneurial class systematically, leaving no one to lead the recovery. This is not about money but about living!

"To increase interest rates to fight inflation is not the solution in 2022!"

Dr. Bak Nguyen & André Châtelain

Within the first months of the pandemic, all of our governments and leaders understood the importance of self-sustaining production in key sectors such as food, drugs, energy, and communication. These systems have to be independent and not be directly linked to any interruption of the supply chain or transport from another part of the world.

The globalization of our supply and production chains emphasized our dependence on the cost of energy (transport), therefore, reflecting directly its impact in the final tag price of every single good. Historically, in Canada, most provincial governments understood the importance of the cost of energy and nationalized the energy industry throughout the country. Many different models emerged from the different local initiatives.

Today, almost the entirety of the production and distribution of energy is owned or under the control of the provincial governments like in the province of Québec. In some provinces, the model adopted was a partnership with the private sector but with the government in control, like in Ontario.

In Québec, that initiative led to the creation of Hydro-Québec in the 40s. 80 years later, the economical and societal model of that initiative made Québec a leader in the management of its domestic energy production. What led to the creation of Hydro-Québec was the unjustified increase of electricity back then. The electricity price is not dictated by free markets but by the evolution of the cost of production and maintenance of its infrastructure. Consequently, Canada is a world champion in keeping the cost of electricity affordable and under control for its citizens.

"By the people, for the people. Twice!"

Dr. Bak Nguyen & André Châtelain

State companies such as Hydro-Québec are very profitable and since it is government-owned, in other words, public owned, the profits go back to the people. Doing so, the people benefit twice from that model, 1 with reasonable and stable energy bills and 2, from the profits of the state agency reinvested in society.

That's a proven working model. Why not include all of the energy sectors in that model, one by the people and for the people? That will sure tame the acceleration of inflation and cut out the abuses and opportunistic elements.

With the discovery of shale gas and the technology available to extract it, Canada owns the 2nd biggest oil reserve in the world. In 2011, with the exploitation of shale gas, the USA became a leading oil-producing country, cutting much of its dependency on foreign petroleum. We have to nationalize that wealth for the people.

"If oil is nationalized, basically, every citizen is richer."

Who will stand against that? Well, our society is made out of diversity and some would say that it is useless to act as such. We should simply ban the consumption of oil to fight global warming. That is an interesting idea but that won't solve our inflation problem as we speak.

Our economical model of production and way of life is far from being oil-free, at least for the foreseeable future. Transport, goods, and even clothes are derived from petroleum. Changes must happen and the transition has to be stable and controlled, for the good of the people, not solely for profits.

THE PLAN

For this to work, we are proposing **THE BUFFER MODEL**, which is the nationalization of the whole energy sector (electricity, solar, wind, petroleum, natural gas, fuel oil, hydrogen, coal, and all future energy alternative sources). By doing so, the nation can centralize the energy interest around the actual energy production and redistribute its wealth and savings to all of the citizens of the country, wherever their province (Canada) or state (USA) has the resource itself or not.

The second reason to have all of the energy centralized (conventional, alternative, and green) is to redistribute the profit of the actual resources to research and finance the development of alternative energy sources, those more aligned with the environment and with the fight against global warming. There is no perfect solution, we will have to solve the actual problems of inflation and dependence from the exterior factors first, then, develop better ways for the future.

How would the nationalization works? Well, the implication of such plans is of national security level importance and we are very aware that the different levels of government (Federal, provincial, state) may all be involved in such a plan. What we are proposing is that the **BUFFER MODEL** is applied as a whole and all the different governments involved will have to apply the plan in the same measure as if it was a whole.

The **BUFFER MODEL** works for a Nation as a whole, so even if the management shall be shared between the different levels of governance, the plan has to act as a sole entity. If we don't, how could we even face a League of Nations as OPEC? So deals and concessions will have to be struck between the different instances of government for the interest of their people, their citizens. And we will have to make sure that they a held accountable by their citizens while executing this plan.

For example, in Quebec, 37% of the petroleum consumption is from the West of Canada and 63% from the USA. That petroleum is then refined locally in Levis and in Montreal. If we imagine the model for Canada, here is a realistic proposition and humble one (we are very aware that the different parties will have different interests and agendas, but all of the parties, to be on that table will have to agree on the first goal of this initiative, which is to be independent, as a country to stabilize the cost of energy, therefore, the baseline of our cost of living).

In Canada, there should be a central Government Society of Energy, let's call it **ENERGY CANADA**. In 2019, the main Canadian energy sources are:

- Oil, 50.1% of the Canadian total energy production with Alberta (80%) and Saskatchewan (9.9%) as leaders.
- Natural Gas, 31.8% of the Canadian total energy production with Alberta (64%) and British Columbia (32%) as leaders.
- Electricity, 8.5% (Hydro, wind, combustible fossils, nuclear) of the Canadian total energy production with Quebec (hydro 21%) and Ontario (17.6%, mainly nuclear plants) as leaders.
- Coal, 5.3% of the Canadian total energy production with British Columbia (48%) and Alberta (35%) as leaders
- Gas plant natural gas liquid (NGPL), 4.3% of the Canadian total energy production (ethane, propane, butane, and isobutane)

That led to the following, all categories combined, considering solely the energy share production reported above. It ranks the provinces as:

1- Alberta with about 61.8% of the national energy production
2- British Columbia with 12.5% of the national energy production
3- Saskatchewan with 5% of the national energy production

The provinces of Québec and Ontario are contributing with 1.7% (Québec with Hydro) and 1.5% (Ontario with mainly nuclear power) of the national energy production.

In the light of such distribution, we advise the headquarters of **ENERGY CANADA** to be located in the energy capital, which should be Calgary in Alberta.

ENERGY CANADA will be managed by an independent board of directors from energy experts from each province of the country. Experts from the different branches of energy would be included on the strategic board.

In 2019, Canada exported 80.6% of its crude oil production and 42.9% of its marketable natural gas. That illustrated that if **ENERGY CANADA** acts as a whole for the country (by the people for the people), the energy sector will not only contribute to stabilize our economy but also a means to enrich all of its people since profits are then returned to the federal government. To put that in perspective, that represents $124.2 billion (2019), $74.3 billion (2020), 119.9 billion (2021).

Putting that in the perspective that COVID expenses were 600 billion, nationalizing the energy sector, increasing our production, and benefiting our population, surely represents a great national hope to counterbalance fear.

The way **ENERGY CANADA** would work is to nationalize the natural resource itself and to partner with the private sector to exploit (extract and produce) the resource itself. **ENERGY CANADA** will then buy all of the production at established and stable prices, and then direct part of it for local consumption and part of it to exportation.

Since energy production is linked closely with inflation and the economy, with the creation of **ENERGY CANADA**, Canada will have the means to create more wealth and may avoid borrowing more money to cover its deficits. But energy production also bears a cost to the environment, that, **ENERGY CANADA** will also have to ensure its responsibility and its legacy for the future generations, thus, re-injecting and investing a big part of its proceeds into the development and sustainability of greener energy.

Its responsibilities would include:

- the harvesting and production of energy
- the national distribution network and infrastructure
- the prices to the customer before local taxes
- the future exploration and exploitation of natural resources
- the management of its partnership with the private sector for the production of energy (that would allow the existing expertise of the private sector to contribute to the new energy model)
- The final sale distribution network should remain private

By owning and controlling the transport and national distribution infrastructure, **ENERGY CANADA** would also have the duty to safely protect the pipeline and the different means to safely transport energy all across the country.

Now, **ENERGY CANADA** by itself will not be enough to balance the price of crude in the free market controlled by OPEC. But even that will be part of the equation. As the price of gas will be fixed and stabilized, we are thinking of $1.05 per litre and stable for a minimum of 18 months, by the time of this writing. If the price of crude barrel drops as it did in 2014, **ENERGY CANADA** will then buy its oil from the international market while keeping local production of its oil for reserve.

That will avoid the precarity and vulnerability of our entrepreneurs in that field since their production will be guaranteed to be bought by **ENERGY CANADA** at the previously fixed price. Then, as OPEC will have to eventually balance their production to balance their own income, the price of the crude barrel should bounce back to a level that would make sense to all parties.

The beauty of this system would be that no matter the international situation, our citizens would not feel as much, the changes or pressure as we are actually feeling with the gas price rising, combined with the prices of almost all the goods leading to a rise in inflation, which comes with a rise in interest rates. Even if the system is not perfect, can you see how better we would be under such circumstances compared to our situation of international hyperinflation of 2022?

To do so, **ENERGY CANADA** is more than just a government agency of energy. It will also constitute a **FUND** to balance and buffer its mechanism of energy in response to the free market of crude. Of course, in times of low crude price, the **FUND** will buy the external oil and even profit from selling it for local consumption while redirecting these profits to support our local production, thus, ensuring for the long term, our independence and domestic energy production.

As mentioned before, by the time of this writing, we estimate that the price at the pump should be fixed at $1.05 per litre and remain stable for the next 18 months. Any price increase will have to be related to the cost of production and transport, not greed or profit.

In the case that the price of crude is high and profitable, **ENERGY CANADA** will sell its reserves and production to foreign countries, making even more profit for the **ENERGY FUND**, the government and its citizens while ensuring the stability of our economic system.

The USA with its reserve of shale gas can become an even bigger producer, combined with their actual domestic production of conventional energy. Its federal agency might be distributed differently but with the same idea in mind, that energy should benefit all of its citizens, no matter the states in which they live in.

In Europe, looking at the confirmed reserve of shale gas, France, the UK, Germany, Poland, Estonia, Latvia, and Lithuania would be able to control their own fate concerning their energy independence and the stability of their economy. Since the European Union is already an organization combining many resources and constituted by independent countries, it will have to negotiate a new alliance, for Europe as a whole, just like the idea and spirit upon which the European Union was founded upon.

This will not be done overnight but it will be a permanent cure to the recurring problem of inflation and recession based on the price of oil, hyperinflation, and high-interest rates. By doing so, we just solved a big part of the issues on our economic table.

Actually, if we apply this model with political will and vision, it might even prevent many future wars from happening, not all, but many.

And before concluding this chapter, we would like your attention on the **HOPE** part of this solution. Well established since the beginning of our journey, Estonia, Latvia, and Lithuania are the most affected by this current crisis.

Well, they might be amongst the wealthiest as they are sitting on an immense reserve of shale gas. If they apply our economic model, they will protect their emerging energy sector from any OPEC offensive. And if they are seeking to share that resource with the rest of Europe, they would also have the protection of the rest of Europe from any invaders, looking to steal their natural resources.

This plan is much more than a philosophical exercise saying what will be great, it will actually solve so many of our existing problems. But first, we need to understand what is at stake; that globalization makes everyone's problem, our problem; and sharing does not mean giving; it means utilizing the strength of every party in the trade.

Join us as we are sharing with you our findings and a solution to avoid the dead-end crisis ahead. This is hope, we still have the time to act, and we have a plan. This is **COVIDCONOMICS, TAMING INFLATION WITHOUT INCREASING INTEREST RATES.**

Welcome to the Alphas.

I REFUSE TO BELIEVE THAT THE ONLY MEANS TO FIGHT INFLATION IS BY RAISING THE INTEREST RATES AND KILLING OUR ENTREPRENEURIAL CLASS IN THE PROCESS
Dr. Bak Nguyen

CHAPTER 5
"THE LIBERTY MODEL"
INTEGRATION AND SUSTAINABILITY

BY Dr. BAK NGUYEN

We gave you all that we had in us, elaborating this plan and illustrating with facts and historical data why and how we came to such a conclusion. I must tell you how proud and happy I am about this journey so far. We gave you everything, for the good of all, for stability, for prosperity and peace!

What a noble conclusion. Not yet. It would be very naive on our part to think that even if we are working for the greater good, that resistance will not stand in the way. This is change, even necessary and urgently needed, with every change will come its toll of resistance.

> **"There is simply no change without resistance. The greater the pain, the less the resistance but resistance, there will always be."**
> Dr. Bak Nguyen

That's unfortunate but I made my peace with that a long time ago. I am an entrepreneur by nature and an agent of change, so I had my experience dealing with change and its implementation.

The first rule was to understand the problem and its causes. We did that extensively. Then, each issue found needs to be addressed, with humility and openness, even if we do not have the perfect solution, yet. That is also done. In doing so, we have established the WHY and the HOW, and the WHY of our HOWs. Now, we have a plan.

Since our intentions were not to build a plan but to see to its application and to benefit with all of you of its consequences, in this case, to tame inflation, to stabilize the interest rates, and to save our already wounded economy, let's spend the rest of this journey on executing this plan.

"To have the idea is simply just the beginning. 90% of the success is in the execution."
Dr. Jean De Serres

That, I learnt from my friend and mentor, Dr. Jean De Serres, former president of Hema-Québec. Well, before executing the plan, we need the support of the people and of the leaders in power. We need to ease the resistance and remain calm and gracious in the process.

I was scratching my head for nights to have something meaningful to write after the last chapter about THE solution. How can we overcome the doubts, the naysayers and those too close-minded to seek a better solution while clearly, what they have in hand isn't working (on that, you won't be reading these lines if you thought that we were doing okay)!

The support of the people! I am not naive and I know that inflation, the economy, globalization, and the free market are not the most popular subjects. I don't blame you, I am one of you. Before feeling the heat of hyperinflation in 2022, I was not concerned either.

I may have reacted more violently than most of you but, I too reacted. In other words, I was late, acting after the facts, and left in damage control mode. In a word, we are late to the game and we do not have much time to face the criticisms, the doubts before it would be too late.

So how could we gain the support of the majority to start implementing the solution and improve upon it as we move forward?

"The support of the people!"

Dr. Bak Nguyen

That was the one and only answer, the support of the people. And how can we make sure of the support of the people through such an endeavour to reform our energy sector and economy? Well, how about having the people benefit a 3rd time from the new equation of energy?

The first benefit was to have a cheaper gas price at the pump (compared to 2022) and one that will stay stable. The second benefit was to send back the profits of such operation to the government for more services to the people.

But that may not be enough. What if the words get lost in translation, over time and space? Since the **LIBERTY MODEL** is one that will oppose us with OPEC, with the actual players of the energy industry and all of the people in the shadow, each with their own agendas, how can we keep the focus on the greater good, of stabilizing the energy sector and to redistribute the benefit to the citizens?

Transparency is the key to that question. Transparency and continuous empowerment. So there is a key ingredient missing from the actual **LIBERTY MODEL**, a key that will ensure that no future player could diverge from its goal or nobility, for whatever excuse.

How about making it into law, from the constitution of the **LIBERTY MODEL** that 20% of the profits will be directly transferred back to its rightful owners, just like shareholders? What I am proposing is to redirect a check, twice a year to each citizen of the country.

Why a check and not a tax credit you might ask? Because a check is clear of all tax filters. I want the people of the right and the left to have a clear message of how their **ENERGY AGENCY** is doing as close as possible to what is unfolding on the ground. That is why I want to deploy a check twice a year, so the citizen is kept close to this wealth and stability model.

This won't just be another title you read in the news and eventually go blind to. This is your legacy and your share of the pie, on top of the first 2 advantages. Receiving a check, twice a year will also keep you motivated to have the right people elected and in management. In other words, as you, the people are motivated and engaged in the system, you are keeping the people in power in your name, accountable, twice a year and not just once every 4 years. That's freedom, power, and money, all from the same solution.

Our energy agency will be acting in a very highly competitive environment, one in which we need the best minds in command. That will require compensating them accordingly and not based on simply government philosophy. Getting a check twice a year, as a shareholder, you will now understand who is worth your trust.

That said, I am also very aware that not all shareholders or citizens will understand the complexity of running such an agency with long-term benefits to protect. That is why, the nomination of its board members will still be under the governance of the executive branch of power, but now, the people will have a better understanding of how their legacy and national wealth are leveraged.

At the round table when we first started this conversation, my son of 12-year-old demanded to be included. Then, after having listened for a long moment to all of these new words and concepts, he asked very politely why don't we engage with the youth and his generation. We were then talking about the shortage of staff.

William then proposed to involve his generation, only, for them to get involved, we need to treat them as partners too, not just ordering them around. We need to stop talking down on them and include them in the plan with words they will relate to.

Well, as we are writing the better version of the future, here's how that would translate. Citizens of all ages should be included and at equal part no matter their gender or age as shareholders. No discrimination! If legally you are a citizen, this is your share, you are a shareholder!

Doing so will engage with our youth from the beginning and teach them the mechanisms of the new economy, one in which they will get involved much sooner than in the present system. They will also have much more time to contribute and improve, maybe even before they come to voting age. That will also engage with another problem faced by our Western societies, our demographic and natality issues. If the wealth of energy does not discriminate amongst its citizens (gender or age), these family with more kids will add up their "dividends" one check per family member. That should empower the natality rate of the country in the right direction while engaging with the next generation right from the start.

That's a lot of money you might say. Well, that money is not money that we are taking away from either the people or the governments. That will all be financed from the profits of the Energy Agency from the **LIBERTY MODEL**. So now, what is not to love in the improved model?

Let's take a minute to summarize the **LIBERTY MODEL** until now:

- Nationalization of the Energy sector as a whole
- Exploitation with the highest respect for the environment since it is now government owned
- Partnership with the private sector
- Stabilization of the inflation and the cost of living (at least those tied with energy cost)
- Resources to finance the greener energy sources

The advantages of the **LIBERTY MODEL** are:

- Stabilization of the inflation
- Stop the increase of interest rate and the FEAR FACTOR
- Lower and stable gas price at the pump compared to 2022
- The creation of national wealth (returns to the government)
- The means to avoid or reduce the risks of future wars (Europe)

And for the citizens as shareholders in the improved model:

- Lower and stable gas price at the pump compared to 2022
- The creation of national wealth (returns to the government)

- Bi-annual dividends in the form of a check to all the citizens without age discrimination
- A means to engage with the youth from a young age
- A means to help reverse the natality problem in Western Countries

And I am just listing the advantages of the side effects of the **LIBERTY MODEL**, I am not selling anything, just looking for a solution to our immediate problems of hyperinflation and recession.

The selling part of this equation came as I was looking for a way to ease the resistance to change. Well, okay, then, I started selling this plan to the people and see how it went. With the improved model, I can't imagine a citizen who would not stand behind me, behind us. Even our side effects are solutions on their own!

Now, it is time to start selling!

"For stability, for prosperity, for peace."

I could add to that, for the future, but that would also mean that the future is always another concept to incorporate. We did that from the DNA of the model, including funds for greener energy and removing the age discrimination from the equation. So, **FOR STABILITY, FOR PROSPERITY, FOR PEACE!**

And the name? The **BUFFER MODEL** is the technical name that explains the true mechanism of our proposed model as imagined

78

by André Châtelain. I put my twist on it, inspired by my own experience and the conversations I had with the Alphas on that round table, François Dufour, Tranie Vo, and William Bak.

Well, if the **BUFFER MODEL** is a technical name, it is not the best. In French, the translation as **LE MODÈLE TAMPON** is the worst branding ever! I went through all the synonyms of **BUFFER** for both languages and couldn't find something appealing enough to the general public.

Then I came back to the tagline, **FOR STABILITY, FOR PROSPERITY, FOR PEACE**. What name will empower such values? As the idea of proposing a bi-annual dividend check to all the citizens without age discrimination is, not only money, but a means to empower them to be more involved in the management of their natural resources and the impact on the future generation, combined with all the immediate advantages of independence to the international oil market controlled by OPEC, the name **LIBERTY MODEL** came as the perfect, brandable name for our model. After all, as mentioned earlier, this is not about money but about life!

THE LIBERTY MODEL
FOR STABILITY, FOR PROSPERITY, FOR PEACE

So what resistance is left? If all of the criticisms of this model go about its name, it would be a straight success. This is really an inclusive plan for every citizen and for a better future. Let's start building!

Join us as we are sharing with you our findings and a solution to avoid the dead-end crisis ahead. This is hope, we still have the time to act, and we have a plan. This is **COVIDCONOMICS, TAMING INFLATION WITHOUT INCREASING INTEREST RATES.**

Welcome to the Alphas.

CHAPTER 6
"SUSTAINABLE DEVELOPMENT"

LASTING IMPACT FOR NOW AND THE FUTURE

BY Dr. BAK NGUYEN & ANDRÉ CHÂTEALAIN

The biggest paradox of this plan is that it requires immediate actions and consequences to change the trends settling as we speak. Not acting or procrastinating with the excuse of finding the perfect plan would be the worst of alternatives. But then, we need a way to fix the weaknesses of our societies or, at least, make sure that this NEW MODEL will not worsen the other parameters of our society.

"ONE PROBLEM AT A TIME."

The Alphas

Our new economic model proposed a way to protect the base of our economy from hyperinflation coming from the ups and downs of the cost of energy. Sure inflation will still be a phenomenon that our societies will have to keep in check but as demonstrated previously, it won't allow such a spiral of hyperinflation to cripple our economy as it is doing in 2022.

What should keep our focus is that until now, we, the people, have very little influence over such waves and are left reacting to save and patch our systems and ways of life. Even our governments alone cannot change the tide of such a phenomenon as we witnessed in 2022. The cure has to be organized and synchronized within the Western countries.

How did we arrive at such a level of dependency and without the means to stir our own destiny? Well, many factors led to our present system but globalization is by far the biggest contributor. Globalization, that's a whole other subject to debate, about its pros and cons. Since we are in a quest to fight hyperinflation and need to act right away, with your permission, let's focus our energy and take home a first victory.

"One victory at a time."

That said, we have followed with clarity the path of hyperinflation and what led to its spiral out of control. Nationalizing our energy sector will help keep the domestic gas price under control but not the cost of transport of goods back and forth around the globe.

Actually, it would if all the Western countries act in symphony to counterbalance the world oil production, therefore, taking control over the oil production and its price internationally. But that too will come at a great cost: the environment.

If we can act in unison and take back control of the price of energy, we still need to know that all of the other countries from our supply chain are keeping their costs under control too! If not, hyperinflation will still affect them and it will spread within the cost of production and quickly move upstream to our tag price as consumers.

In other words, as the Western countries are counter-balancing OPEC, we will be exporting oil on the global market. On that, looking at the shale gas reserves, North America and Europe have more than enough reserves to control their own fate in energy. Here are 3 maps of Canada, the USA, and Europe with estimated shale gas reserves:

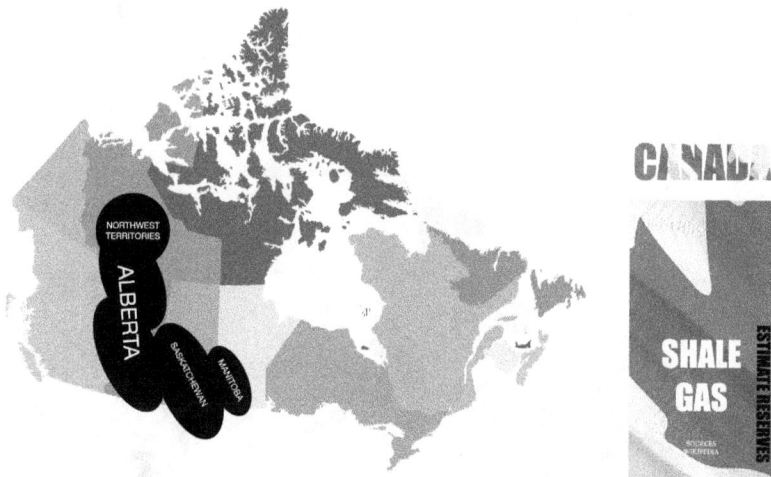

In Canada, 3 provinces and 1 territory have shale gas in their soil: Alberta, Saskatchewan, Manitoba, and the Northwest Territories.

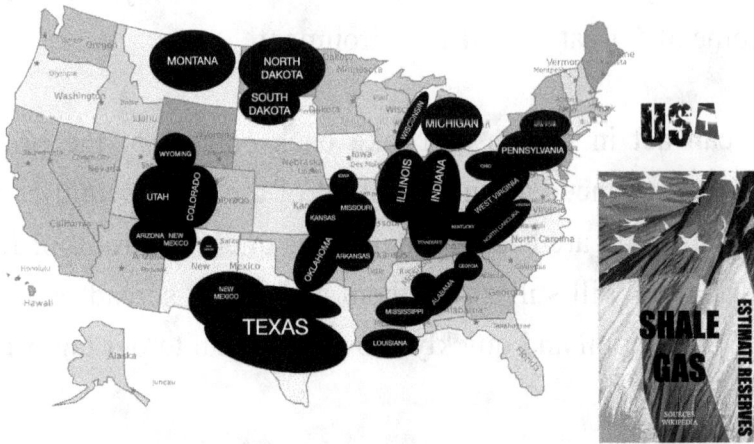

In the USA, 30 states are estimated to have shale gas in their soil: Montana, North Dakota, South Dakota, Wyoming, Utah, Colorado, Arizona, New Mexico, Texas, Oklahoma, Kansas, Iowa, Missouri, Arkansas, Illinois, Wisconsin, Michigan, Indiana, Tennessee, Mississippi, Louisiana, Alabama, Georgia, Kentucky, West Virginia, Virginia, North Carolina, Ohio, Pennsylvania, and New York.

In Europe, 14 countries are estimated to have shale gas in their soil: the United Kingdom, France, Germany, Poland, Belgium, Netherlands, Denmark, Norway, Sweden, Estonia, Latvia, Lithuania, and Greece.

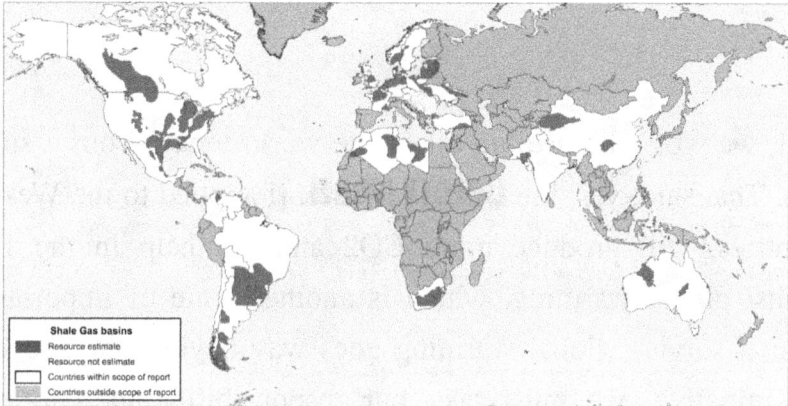

Shale Gas basins
- Resource estimate
- Resource not estimate
- Countries within scope of report
- Countries outside scope of report

SOURCE: WIKIPEDIA

These maps have been recreated from a map on Wikipedia as the source for the world's shale gas reserves estimated. These prove that if the Western countries stand united in a common front in the **ENERGY FRONT**, we can regularize the world production of oil and really keep hyperinflation under control.

That said, the economy shall resume but our biggest criticism will come from the environmentalists on the energy exploitation and the increase of released CO_2. And not all countries in the Globalisation supply chain have the same principles and environmental norms. As said before, one of the side effects of globalization is that we do not have direct influence over how a country is governed.

"In other words, our values and principles are averaged with those part of our supply chain."

Dr. Bak Nguyen

Well, we won't be healing all of the world today, from a single plan. That said, yes, the **LIBERTY MODEL**, if applied to the Western countries, will produce more CO_2 and not help in the fight against global warming, which is another issue of importance. Even if solving global warming goes way beyond the scope of this initiative, we must take our responsibility and, at least, counterbalance our footprint on the environment.

This is why we are proposing a scoring system that will take into account the CO_2 released and will have to finance environmental initiatives to clean the planet as we are moving forward. Not in 10 years, but right away, with the same urgency.

How will we tackle such colossal tasks while saving the world economy you might ask? Well, the **LIBERTY MODEL** takes care of what is inside of a country. Since the **MODEL** will tame hyperinflation and transfer the saving to the customers, bringing the price of goods to a more reasonable level, **GLOBALIZATION** will also need to do its share.

The environmental cost of moving raw materials and finished goods back and forth has its cost, and in more ways than in the tag price. Since not all countries will have the same environmental priorities and treaties will take forever to standardize the world supply chain, we propose a custom importation fee for the goods from all countries, even in free trade zones. That new custom fees will go 100% to international environmental initiatives like cleaning the oceans (for example).

The **CUSTOM FEES** will be managed by each country but cannot diverge from international issues. Until now, that could cause a big problem as ships from all countries can travel the ocean and international waters, and yet, no single government has the authority to regulate nor safeguard that natural resource. We are limited by our international borders and frontiers, which are only legal and valid on paper, but not in the grand scheme of the planet.

Having the **GLOBALIZATION DUTY** at the importation is not protectionism as the critics will be screaming their lungs out. 100% of the duty collected is directed to finance international environmental issues! This is just us taking our responsibility and leading the way to sustainable development.

By the end of the day, these fees will be transferred back to the customers which may not feel such a burden since that price will still be cheaper than if it was hit by hyperinflation. Our goal is not to tax nor to create more governing structures, but to assume our responsibility, and start balancing our environmental footprint.

"We cannot simply take and take forever without consequences."

Dr. Bak Nguyen

And what about the national environmental issues? Those will be addressed with the profit budgeted within the **LIBERTY MODEL** for environmental issues and green energy research.

The importance that we would like to stretch here is that, even if we won't be solving all of the environmental issues related to the production of energy, its consumption or the side effects of globalization, it is of prime importance to keep our systems in check and with the respect of the environment we are harvesting from.

Hyperinflation is a fire that spreads faster than wildfire. Well, we should act now and act firmly. Global warming is more patient and it is still buffering our blindness and excess until the planet would not absorb nor tolerate anymore. Then, we might not have enough time to react. Let's take hyperinflation as a warning, and take the opportunity to fix some of our major issues.

As shown in the maps, we have the resources, we have the technology. What may have lacked were the courage and political will to stand up and seize our destiny. We can take back the control of our way of life and tame the beast of hyperinflation, and our responsibility towards the planet, towards our children and grandchildren. The time of debates and excuses is over. We must act, now!

Join us as we are sharing with you our findings and a solution to avoid the dead-end crisis ahead. This is hope, we still have the time to act, and we have a plan. This is **COVIDCONOMICS, TAMING INFLATION WITHOUT INCREASING INTEREST RATES.**

Welcome to the Alphas.

I REFUSE TO BELIEVE THAT THE ONLY MEANS TO FIGHT INFLATION IS BY RAISING THE INTEREST RATES AND KILLING OUR ENTREPRENEURIAL CLASS IN THE PROCESS
Dr. Bak Nguyen

CHAPTER 7
"THE BUTTERFLY EFFECT"
SUCCESS, RESISTANCE & TRENDS

BY Dr. BAK NGUYEN

We spent the first half of this book understanding the problem of hyperinflation and its consequences. We elaborated a plan to solve, at its sources hyperinflation. Inflation will still be a phenomenon, but one our systems proved it can handle as seen in the pandemic crisis from 2020 to the beginning of 2022 as the wars took over.

The solution isn't perfect but it will release the pressure off of the central banks to keep increasing interest rates and kill our entrepreneurial class in the process. Please keep in mind that inflation is the phenomenon that happens as demand exceeds production.

Well, we don't want to decrease demand, we stalled production in the management of the pandemic, and that led to a world production and supply chain already crippled, despite all of the efforts of the entrepreneurs and governments. Please don't adjust demand to balance it with the crippled production.

That will not be a cure but the amputation of the other leg to balance with the wounded one. That is a violent image but it is exactly what it is, to slow down demand by drying credit and injecting fear into the system.

In chapter 5, we proposed that 20% of the profit will be directly sent to the citizens without age discrimination, twice a year. Well, let's cover the 80% of the profit left on the table and how it will be utilized:

- 20% go to the government and the national budget
- 20% to keep growing the National Agency
- 20% to feed the **ENERGY FUND** to support domestic production against an offensive of OPEC (lowering their price below our production cost). In the case of a prolonged offensive, the Federal Government will have to invest more money to assure 100% stability in the protection of domestic energy production.
- 20% towards environmental initiatives and green energy research.

Even if the proportion can vary from one year to the next after careful study by the board of directors, the profit paid in dividends of 20% to the citizens CAN NOT change. This is to keep the citizens close to the management of their legacy and natural resources.

This plan is not perfect, we are fully aware of that. That said, this is a plan that we need to adopt right now to tame hyperinflation before irreversible damages occur in our economy and send it into the worst economic depression of all time, with perfect storm conditions: **COST OF ENERGY**, **HYPERINFLATION**, and **HIGH-INTEREST RATES**.

We cannot afford to repeat history and then, read about it in the next History book. We must act now. We have the means, the knowledge, and the time to do so.

"To each decision, each action, a new cascade of elements will emerge with its pros and cons."

These changes that we are proposing will come with their toll in objections and opposition. To each change, its opposition. So let's do that, let's borrow from the opposition, the resistance, to criticize the butterfly effects of the **LIBERTY MODEL**, and address its flaws right away, or at least, identify the weaknesses that still need improvement.

OPEC

The **LIBERTY MODEL** will oppose the actual oil producers and OPEC. Well, the response of OPEC whether they increase or decrease their oil production is built-in as a part of the equation, at its base with the **ENERGY FUND**.

Actually, if they raise the price of crude, everyone, including us will be richer from our oil exportation. If they keep the price low, they will hurt themselves much more and they will be transferring their reserve to us at a much cheaper price. They will not affect our domestic oil production as they had in the past. The **LIBERTY MODEL** is assuring the stability of our economy whatever the price of oil on the international free market.

OILS PRODUCERS

About the private sector of oil production, well, some will always be opposed to any change, whatsoever, especially those who are losing monopolistic-like positions. To be fair, the government could buy them out, just like governments did in the past when they nationalized the electricity sector. The other option for them is to partner up with the **NATIONAL ENERGY AGENCY** and sell their production to the federal government. They lost control but still have access to safe and stable profits if they decide to stay in the new economical model.

Let's not forget that the **LIBERTY MODEL** will also allow the emergence of a whole new legion of energy entrepreneurs as seen in the USA from 2000 to 2014 utilizing the new technologies to extract shale gas. Those were the ones hit by the OPEC offensive back then. Not anymore.

The **LIBERTY MODEL** is built with the idea of partnering with the private sector, what is nationalized is the natural resources, not the production itself.

ENVIRONMENTALISTS

People being people and experts being experts, we predict that the **LIBERTY MODEL** will have a great approval rate, especially as the citizens start receiving their dividend checks. After the initial time to set up and stabilize the nationalization process and establish its national distribution throughout the country, profits will come. If you have any doubt, please visit Dubai and see their wonders standing as a testimony of their wealth, energy wealth.

But then, our experts will want to export more and more. The people will be supporting since their dividend checks will increase proportionally. What about global warming and the reduction of CO_2 emissions?

> **"To win, one needs both mindset and money.**
> **Money without mindset is useless**
> **and so are mindset without money."**
> William Bak

That's what William discovered by playing strategy games on his laptop. Well, after decades of telling the world that global warming is a threat, we are still making plans for the future, with a transition period. According to the experts, it might be too little too late. They have the knowledge, took decades to start accumulating political will. Well, to be honest, they are still fighting for the issue.

I thanked them for their fortitude and the objections they will have about our plan to save our economy. And they are right doing so. One crisis at a time! What the **LIBERTY MODEL** is bringing to the table is the **URGENCY** to act now, hyperinflation will hurt us much sooner than global warming, with all due respect.

Its implementation might takes months and years while, in the meantime, our governments can already start selling their oil on the international market with great profit. The USA are already doing so with the release of 1 million barrel per day for the next 6 months.

Canada is ready to do so too. Actually, the Prime Minister of Alberta, Jason Kenney is pleading to the Federal Government to allow the removal, or at least, the raising of the cap of production imposed on the oil producers. In his view, this is a great opportunity to export and sell oil at great profit. And he is right on that issue! Can you see the paradox? As the world is fearful of inflation and recession, this could be a time of prosperity! Still not convinced? Take a trip to Dubai and see what are their plans and hopes. The **LIBERTY MODEL** erases the line between us and OPEC, as we all join the same side, as oil producers.

That will be even more alarming to the environmentalists and the scientific community and we agree. But not doing so, our global warming issues are still left unattended and I doubt that OPEC will be acting to help with their profits.

We encouraged the involvement of those fighting global warming to be at the table, not to stall this initiative but to know what to do as soon as money flows, and it will, much sooner than you might expect. They have the "**MINDSET**" to borrow from William's words. Soon, we will have the means. And about the political will? Well, within the **LIBERTY MODEL**, keeping our independence in energy is the primary goal. Reinvesting for the future comes right after.

"For stability, for prosperity, for peace."
Dr. Bak Nguyen

Just like I said before, **THE FUTURE** is not a concept but a primal component of our equation. Now, listening to the environmentalists and scientific community, we must give back more than we take. And we must do that for yesterday!

The **LIBERTY MODEL** will bring money in much sooner than any other alternative now in place, still late, but the fastest. Then, talking about investing in research and green energy, those will take decades to bear fruits, if they succeed.

I will apply here the same conviction and sense of urgency that we had fighting hyperinflation. Forget about green energy, at least for now. Let's finance these scientists with immediate solutions to clean the planet. Everything environment related is fair game. The idea is to balance our footprint on nature, and on that, we are so far behind.

The **LIBERTY MODEL** will accentuate our footprint on nature, that is why we will (not must but will) act as quickly and with the same determination. The time of thinking and arguing is over, let's act and see results.

The first goal would be to finance these initiatives with immediate impact. The selection of initiatives will be based on such factors, keeping the score of how much footprints we left versus what we cleaned. And the environmentalists will keep track to influence the next initiatives. This is not replacing what our governments are currently doing but comes as a reinforcement. With the wealth coming with the **LIBERTY MODEL**, our environmentalists just gain a **STRIKE FORCE** well funded and sustained for the foreseeable future.

Contrary to the current model where initiatives take months and years for approval and then, run out of money, the **LIBERTY STRIKE FORCE** is one with the will to balance its footprint (until it can clean more than it is taking) and one, perpetually funded by our **ENERGY AGENCY**. The conditions for the renewal of the initiatives will always be based on the footprint score and the other alternatives on the table, but money and the will are there.

In a few words, the **LIBERTY MODEL** just provides a new arm to the guardians of our planet, with the **LIBERTY STRIKE FORCE**.

"For stability, for prosperity, for peace."

So what else? What resistance haven't we addressed? Actions have consequences and so are inactions, no matter how small. I am very aware that the **LIBERTY MODEL** is not perfect but it can do much good in the short and mid-term, as we keep our minds open to improve on its model and its integrations.

This chapter just proves how powerful and inclusive it can be. With the mission to balance its footprint and its dividend mechanism, the **LIBERTY MODEL** is a new model of economy and of democracy, one self-sustaining, one close to the population, and one making and bridging the future in the present tense. Now the **LIBERTY** name reveals the depth of its values and what it stands for.

Join us as we are sharing with you our findings and a solution to avoid the dead-end crisis ahead. This is hope, we still have the time to act, and we have a plan. This is **COVIDCONOMICS, TAMING INFLATION WITHOUT INCREASING INTEREST RATES.**

Welcome to the Alphas.

I REFUSE TO BELIEVE THAT THE ONLY MEANS
TO FIGHT INFLATION IS BY RAISING THE INTEREST RATES
AND KILLING OUR ENTREPRENEURIAL CLASS IN THE PROCESS
Dr. Bak Nguyen

PART 2
HOPE & FEAR

CHAPTER 8
"ANDRÉ CHÂTELAIN"
BY ANDRÉ CHÂTELAIN

In the last few days, I have been invited to reflect on the different problems that our societies are facing, all more urgent than the other (inflation, raising interest rates, cost of energy, the rigged free market of oil…).

I must say that it was very stimulating to exchange ideas and to discuss openly at that round table of the Alphas. Together, as a team, we arrived, with our analysis, conclusion, and proposed solution to limit the damages and economical risk of system failure at the national, continental and international levels.

For the last 20 years, I studied with interest the evolution of our society and of other western countries (France, USA, etc.) The dynamism and capability to execute of the different governments have greatly diminished year after year.   The possibility of arriving at structuring great endeavours is now against most odds (the opposition, the explosion of cost, the weight of management and legal, etc…)

I witness more and more division of our population on all the possible topics. It's almost like to object is now a must not to be missed on. It seems that it became more important to criticize than to build philosophies and endeavours for the greater good and the future generations.

No matter what the endeavours and ideas are about, to protest and to show our discontentment is now king and cool! And the media keep fuelling that image and false fame. Which, sadly, leads to the paralysis of actions. Creative and energetic entrepreneurship is simply crushed by that pressure, increasingly present in all spheres of our society.

As for a result, we are stalling, even when faced with national and international challenges that menace our way and standard of living. Instead of empowering the needed change, we are discouraging those capable for making the difference, of leading the difference for all of us.

In our book, we offer courageous solutions that could certainly improve our lives in Canada and elsewhere in the world, not to some but to all its citizens. Some will be in favour and will say: that's a great idea, let's give it a try!

Others, opposed to the idea, will stage massive protests to bully our politicians to close their eyes and turn their attention elsewhere. Unfortunately, our politicians are most likely to follow the immediate popularity of their decisions, not always to weigh the consequences over time. Their focus is, therefore, always on the short-term and the electoral cycles. It is certainly not the best way to build and develop a country, any country.

Consequently, we stop embracing the new ideas that could propel us forward and not to keep repeating the same mistake over and over again. All of that in the fear of displeasing a minority, the majority having lost their voice and becoming silent over time...

Being an optimistic person and a firm believer in people and their ability to make a difference, I hope that we will be able to evolve our political system in order to eliminate the opposition syndrome that has persisted for too long in our society. We have to ensure that all elected officials, regardless of their political allegiance, will work together for the well-being of the country.

When our legislative and political rules are modernized, we will be amazed at our ability to attract more and more capable, knowledgeable and skilled people to all our levels of governance. The country, the future and your constituents need your talent, your will to make a difference and your passion.

Hoping that my words have moved some if not most of you, I am convinced that we are capable to stand up for our values and our beliefs to grow back into a society rich and creative, respectful and grateful, not only for our own good but for the future generations too. Great things we can and we must do. Together we can build the bridges for a better future, to all! Until then, this is my humble contribution to this book, to our society, to you. I hope that it helped you to understand the different facets of our economy, especially why things are not working as we speak.

"The beginning of every solution starts with comprehending the problem in the first place."

André Châtelain

Join us as we are sharing with you our findings and a solution to avoid the dead-end crisis ahead. This is hope, we still have the time to act, and we have a plan. This is **COVIDCONOMICS, TAMING INFLATION WITHOUT INCREASING INTEREST RATES.**

Welcome to the Alphas.

I REFUSE TO BELIEVE THAT THE ONLY MEANS TO FIGHT INFLATION IS BY RAISING THE INTEREST RATES AND KILLING OUR ENTREPRENEURIAL CLASS IN THE PROCESS
Dr. Bak Nguyen

CHAPTER 9
"FRANÇOIS DUFOUR"
BY FRANÇOIS DUFOUR

We all aspire to have a better quality of life, not only for ourselves but for our family and community. One may ponder on how to improve our society to achieve the above-mentioned objectives. Those are my hopes.

Is it by improving government policies? Is it by reducing the size of the government in terms of jurisdiction and resources? In this book, we talked about adding another government intervention to the prices of oil. Given the dire situation, we are forced to go in this direction. Ultimately the government should be there as a last resort, such as the subprime bailouts, Canadian emergency relief benefits, and protecting us during wartimes.

The size of the government should always be controlled and maintained at a certain level, a controlled level. We saw over time that having one institution with most of the power and resources will lead to inequalities and corruption. Human beings must be left to their own demise.

"Individual ambition and entrepreneurship are far more powerful than the community aspect."

François Dufour

We saw clearly with the cold war the dualities of two philosophies, and one ended up being the definitive victor. Moreover, economically speaking a basic principle such as the dead weight loss, where there is an inherent loss of resources when government and taxation are involved.

To increase overall wealth, the interventions of the government should, if possible, be reduced. Just like antibiotics, the government should only be involved when needed. But today we are facing major challenges in our economy that will lead to societal and political turmoil as inflation is slowly creeping into the food price.

"When the people are hungry this is where we see civil unrest."

François Dufour

The government needs to act now and very swiftly. Raising interest rates might not be the best solution as it never is. This new economic mechanism is a solution. Indeed, with the information highway, capitalism is on steroids and moves quickly.

An event in China can impact the economy in Canada the next day. Raising the interest rate is a slow-moving action that will impact people but in a rather mid to long-term timeframe. One might say that raising the interest rates is not enough timely and is based on inflation numbers which are a lagging indicator, lagging by at least 6 months. One fast and efficient solution is to control the price of oil today.

Are we on the right path? Is the way we manage the globalized economy the most beneficial for the welfare of society and the environment as a whole? Those are some of the questions we will discuss in another book. A lot must be reexamined, such as the delocalization of factories and jobs, tax evasion, and inequalities.

Join us as we are sharing with you our findings and a solution to avoid the dead-end crisis ahead. This is hope, we still have the time to act, and we have a plan. This is **COVIDCONOMICS, TAMING INFLATION WITHOUT INCREASING INTEREST RATES.**

Welcome to the Alphas.

I REFUSE TO BELIEVE THAT THE ONLY MEANS
TO FIGHT INFLATION IS BY RAISING THE INTEREST RATES
AND KILLING OUR ENTREPRENEURIAL CLASS IN THE PROCESS
Dr. Bak Nguyen

CHAPTER 10
"WILLIAM BAK"
BY WILLIAM BAK

I am William Bak, the youngest Alpha at the table. I guess, I am the youngest in the world! I am 12 years old and I will stand for my generation at this table.

A little something about me, I am maybe 12 but I am one of my dad's most productive co-author. I co-signed with my father, Dr. Bak, 34 books already, I also wrote one by myself, so that brings me to 35 books in total! This one is my 36th! I hope that I gained your interest.

I asked to be at the table as I heard my dad talking with the different Alphas. I thought that all I had to do was to talk. Well, it did not happen exactly as planned. First, I had to listen much more than I talked, and then, I was asked to write a chapter about my hope and fear for our economy. Economy, that is still a new word to me!

Honestly, I am worried about the stores, the companies, and the price of gas. From what I can see, the stores are missing a lot of workers as mega stores like Walmart are now forced to close all of the cashiers for self-cashier only. I thought that they were cheap but no, my dad told me that they were forced to do so. That is a strange feeling to shop nowadays.

About the companies, I saw and heard businesses closing here and there. I heard friends of my dad talking about how hard things are after 2 years and a half in pandemic. I am worried about my parents' company since nobody wants to come back to work in the city anymore... that worries me and there is nothing that I can do about it.

And the gas price is the least of my worries but my dad says that the prices are going up quickly. He even told me the story that when he was about my age the price of gas was about $0.39. Today it is almost $2! That is not a lot at all! Okay, that was a long time ago, but still! Where would it go next?

I know that Alphas around the world are doing their best to fix the situation. My hopes are that we find a way that all cars run on electricity since gas is expensive and also pollutes the planet. I am worried that in 50 years or more, we won't have enough food and that the planet will die and we with it!

I hope also that companies and businesses go back to normal, with people coming back to work in the city and inside the stores. This madness has to end soon!

To everyone, I deeply hope that we can find a way to motivate ourselves to find back our passion and some pleasure at work. No one seems to be happy at work anymore, they all seem tired, impatient; some, even, angry. Just like the lyrics of the song from The Score, we need to come back, stronger than before!

And finally, my hope is that future generations would never have to face the same problems as today. So this is my chapter and I went all out to write what was in my heart. I am 12 and don't underestimate me. I am here to help!

Join us as we are sharing with you our findings and a solution to avoid the dead-end crisis ahead. This is hope, we still have the time to act, and we have a plan. This is **COVIDCONOMICS, TAMING INFLATION WITHOUT INCREASING INTEREST RATES.**

Welcome to the Alphas.

I REFUSE TO BELIEVE THAT THE ONLY MEANS
TO FIGHT INFLATION IS BY RAISING THE INTEREST RATES
AND KILLING OUR ENTREPRENEURIAL CLASS IN THE PROCESS
Dr. Bak Nguyen

CHAPTER 11
"TRANIE VO"
BY TRANIE VO

My name is Tranie Vo, I am Mdex & Co.'s COO. I have been a woman entrepreneur of diversity for the last 20 years. I co-founded my company with my partner, Dr. Bak. My role in the enterprise is to manage the teams and to develop new markets. I love what I do.

The inflation that we have been experiencing lately has affected everyone without exception. Prices are going up and up, and I'm not just talking about the gas price. This is a major problem that worries everyone.

These last two years, and I am not speaking only for myself, but on the behalf of all the entrepreneurs I met, have been extremely difficult. We've been through all sorts of challenges, from COVID restrictions to mandatory investments for infection control, to the loss of business because people have left their workplaces, to labour shortages. And the list is still long...

Life has changed. People have changed. Some have left and will not come back. Others became bitter and angry... everything has changed. And with these changes, consumer habits followed too. In short, for the entrepreneurial class, the last 2 years have been a real headache and blindfold endurance race! So it was extremely difficult, I won't lie to you.

Personally, I consider myself very lucky to have my team in these stormy times. We have people who believe in us and who are ready to take on the challenges for us and us for them. It's really that team spirit that kept my spirits up and on track over the past 2 years. And now, after the pandemic and the labour shortage, hyperinflation and exploding interest rates are threatening us at our doors. It is not only the rise in rates but also the drying up of consumer credits that affects us.

And this latest wave of attacks can be traced back to the cost of energy. In this journey of **COVIDCONOMICS**, it has been very well illustrated that the price of gas is at the root of our hyperinflation problems. Everything is more expensive, from gas to groceries. This is in addition to the labour shortage which had already caused wages to skyrocket. The explosion in prices will accentuate the vicious cycle of increases...

And the energy factor has simply exploded the already dire situation since the beginning of 2022. On the Alphas' round table, we have a National, North American and European plan to counter hyperinflation. It fits and it makes sense. As far as I can see, it's the only real solution on the table. The chance we have is that we have natural resources, so it is now a question of developing and implementing strategic and economic plans.

In other words, it is possible to reverse this dire situation to make it into a good opportunity to enrich the whole country, or at least, to stop our state of economic siege.

To do so will require leadership and courage from our elected officials. Let's stop having our living conditions dictated by other countries! The answer lies in energy independence.

As an entrepreneur, that gives me a lot of hope. The hope that it is possible to stop our descent into hell, which has been only accelerating since the beginning of this year. For any problem, there is always a solution. Now, we have one! Like our entrepreneurs and workers in the field, we must regain hope and the desire to unite for a solution. My greatest fear is to witness a lack in leadership, courage and/or procrastination that will only worsen our current situation.

Our leaders must prioritize. Yes, there are other problems, but this one, hyperinflation, needs to be brought under control today! And the answer, you have it in this book! It is now a work of leadership to unite our citizens towards a common future, a better one. This economic siege already lasted for more than 2 and a half years. My wish is that, in addition to a solution to these consecutive crises, we also find a way to inner peace and a joy of living. I will refer to Mdex's tagline:

"For joy, for life"

Mdex & Co.

Join us as we are sharing with you our findings and a solution to avoid the dead-end crisis ahead. This is hope, we still have the time to act, and we have a plan. This is **COVIDCONOMICS, TAMING INFLATION WITHOUT INCREASING INTEREST RATES.**

Welcome to the Alphas.

CONCLUSION

BY Dr. BAK NGUYEN

We promised you a plan, here it is. One that will fix hyperinflation at its source. We still have the time to act but for that, we must come together and to set our difference and our own personal agendas aside. If we want out of this crisis, from the menace of the greatest recession of our lifetime, this is our shot.

We are very aware that our plan is not perfect but it is applicable now and will have positive effects for generations to come, for as long as we keep the profit back to the mechanism of the **LIBERTY MODEL:**

1. To give the **LIBERTY** dividends (20%) twice a year without age discrimination to keep the citizens engaged.
2. To buffer and protect our domestic energy production with the **LIBERTY FUND** (20%). Even if the Government may have to inject more money into this FUND in time of crisis, it is a much better bargain than to bail out our economy from hyperinflation and care for the unemployment needs following.

3. To balance our footprint on the Environment in the present tense (20%). The **LIBERTY STRIKE FORCE** is not branding, but a team of operatives perpetually funded with the profits of the **LIBERTY MODEL**, and acting with the same sense of urgency!

These accounted for 60% of the profits of the ENERGY AGENCY. Another 20% will go back to the government and the last 20% to reinvest in the AGENCY infrastructure and evolution, that is basic business management.

The **LIBERTY MODEL** is one that will fix hyperinflation in the short term. It may not be the miracle pill for everything else we are facing, but it is a chance for us to all come together and to stir back our society in the right direction. It is a beacon of hope that we can act, that we can make a difference, that we have the choice to do so or to turn away.

To me, this is more than hope, it is a plan. I wrote this plan because I had the chance to exchange with brilliant people with huge hearts. André, François, Tranie, and William, thank you for your involvement, vision and fortitude. I put everything I had on the table because I felt concerned and I refused to stomach another failure, another defeat; because I refuse to find someone to blame later on.

Now that the goals are clear, that the plan is on the table, can we come together and act in everyone's interest? Sure, there will be intense discussions between the different levels of government regarding the management and control of the AGENCY, we are not naive. Well, they have a month or so to find common ground because, by the end of the day, they are there to represent the interests of their fellow citizens, those who elected them and who will keep them in power. Time is of the essence here!

If Canada and the USA will have to come up with such an agreement between the Provinces and the Federal government, the States and the Central government, there is hope for Europe and its country members. Remember that we are facing a **LEAGUE OF NATIONS, OPEC**. The only way to win this uphill battle is to act as one, as the Western World united for all its citizens.

My hope for the future is to have helped defuse the greatest economical depression of our lifetime. If by doing so, we have helped to build a beacon of hope to fix our other problems such as Global Warming, I do believe that more brilliant minds will be proposing solutions inspired from this model. After all, it is our planet, our lives and our future that are at stake! We do not claim to be the solution to Global Warming, but we sure hope to be a **STRIKE FORCE** in the present tense.

And about my fears? Well, I didn't write a book to just write another book. Which, by the way, will become a documentary that will be submitted to AMAZON PRIME for international distribution. On the matter, I just received a few confirmations and the green light of my production team. I wrote this plan because I believe and I am convinced that we can do it, together. My biggest fear will be to be here, with you, in 5 years, to tell you: "I told you so!". That would be such a shame and a waste because we had a plan and the time to act then.

Well, guess what, we still can. I gave you my heart and my brain, my words and my leadership in this plan. I promise you that I will push for this plan to see life with the means at my disposal. But I can't do this one alone, I need you, all of you to join, to ask questions, to improve our model, to feel concerned and to pressure our decision-makers to make the difference in the present tense.

"For stability, for prosperity, for peace."

Dr. Bak Nguyen

This is not a conclusion but the beginning of a solution, an inclusive one with the ambition, not to be perfect but one to be in the present tense, one to stand as a beacon that change is possible at our level, that citizenship comes with power and inheritance, duty and vision.

We can fix this if we come together. We can avoid the pain and misery ahead if we come together. So join me, for stability, for prosperity, for peace!

We have a plan! This is **COVIDCONOMICS, TAMING INFLATION WITHOUT INCREASING INTEREST RATES.**

Welcome to the Alphas.

I REFUSE TO BELIEVE THAT THE ONLY MEANS
TO FIGHT INFLATION IS BY RAISING THE INTEREST RATES
AND KILLING OUR ENTREPRENEURIAL CLASS IN THE PROCESS
Dr. Bak Nguyen

ANNEX

GLOSSARY OF Dr. BAK's LIBRARY

1

1SELF -080

REINVENT YOURSELF FROM ANY CRISIS
BY Dr. BAK NGUYEN

1SELF is about reinventing yourself to rise from any crisis. Written in the midst of the COVID war, now more than ever, we need hope and the know-how to bridge the future. More than just the journey of Dr. Bak, this time, Dr. Bak is sharing his journey with mentors and people who built part of the world as we know it. Interviewed in this book, CHRISTIAN TRUDEAU, former CEO and FOUNDER of BCE EMERGIS (BELL CANADA), he also digitalized the Montreal Stock Exchange. RON KLEIN, American Innovator, inventor of the magnetic stripe of the credit card, of MLS (Multi-listing services) and the man who digitalized WALL STREET bonds markets.ANDRE CHATELAIN, former first vice-president of the MOVEMENT DESJARDINS. Dr. JEAN DE SERRES, former CEO of HEMA QUEBEC. These men created billions in values and have changed our lives, even without us knowing. They all come together to share their experiences and knowledge to empower each and everyone to emerge stronger from this crisis, from any crisis.

A

AFTERMATH -063
BUSINESS AFTER THE GREAT PAUSE
BY Dr. BAK NGUYEN & Dr. ERIC LACOSTE

In AFTERMATH, Dr. Bak joins forces with Community leader and philanthrope Dr. Eric Lacoste. Two powerful minds and forces of nature in the reaction to the worst economic meltdown in modern times. We are all victims of the CORONA virus. Both just like humans have learnt to adapt to survive, so is our economy. Most business structures and management philosophies are inherited from the age of industrialization and beyond. COVID-19 has shot down the world economy for months. At the time of the AFTERMATH, the truth is many corporations and organizations will either have to upgrade to the INFORMATION AGE or disappear. More than the INFORMATION upgrade, the era of SOCIAL MEDIA and the MILLENNIALS are driving a revolution in the core philosophy of all organizations. Profit is not king anymore, support is. In this time and age where a teenager with a social account can compete with the million dollars PR firm, social implication is now the new cornerstone. Those who will adapt will prevail and prosper, while the resistance and old guards will soon be forgotten as fossils of a past era.

ALPHA DENTISTRY vol. 1 -104
DIGITAL ORTHODONTIC FAQ
BY Dr. BAK NGUYEN

In ALPHA DENTISTRY, DIGITAL ORTHODONTICS FAQ, Dr. Bak is looking to democratize the science of dentistry, starting with orthodontics. In a word, he is sharing everything a patient needs to know on the matter in FAQ form. In order to make the knowledge complete and universal, Dr. Bak has invited Alpha Dentists from all around the world to join in and answer the same question. With Alpha Dentists from America and Europe, ALPHA DENTISTRY is the first effort to create a universal knowledge in the field of dentistry, starting with orthodontics. ALPHA DENTISTRY, DIGITAL ORTHODONTICS FAQ is in response to the COVID crisis, the shortage of staff crisis, and the effort to unify dentistry to the Information Age, as discussed in RELEVANCY and COVIDCONOMICS, THE DENTAL INDUSTRY.

ALPHA DENTISTRY vol. 1 -109
DIGITAL ORTHODONTIC FAQ ASSEMBLED EDITION

🇺🇸 USA 🇪🇸 SPAIN 🇩🇪 GERMANY 🇮🇳 INDIA 🇨🇦 CANADA

BY Dr. BAK NGUYEN, Dr. PAUL OUELLETTE, Dr. PAUL DOMINIQUE, Dr. MARIA KUNSTADTER, Dr. EDWARD J. ZUCKERBERG, Dr. MASHA KHAGHANI, Dr. SUJATA BASAWARAJ, Dr. ALVA AURORA, Dr. JUDITH BÄUMLER, and Dr. ASHISH GUPTA

In ALPHA DENTISTRY, DIGITAL ORTHODONTICS FAQ, Dr. Bak is democratizing the science of dentistry, starting with orthodontics. In a word, he is sharing everything a patient needs to know on the matter in FAQ form, simple words you'll understand.10 International Alpha Doctors, from USA, Spain, Germany, India, and Canada are joining forces to make the knowledge complete and universal. ALPHA DENTISTRY is the first effort to create a universal knowledge in the field of dentistry, this is the orthodontics volume. This is the most ambitious book project in the History of Dentistry. ALPHA DENTISTRY is in response to the COVID crisis, the shortage of staff crisis, and the effort to unify dentistry to the Information Age, as discussed in RELEVANCY and COVIDCONOMICS, THE DENTAL INDUSTRY.

ALPHA DENTISTRY vol. 1 -113
DIGITAL ORTHODONTIC FAQ INTERNATIONAL EDITION

🇺🇸 ENGLISH 🇪🇸 SPANISH 🇩🇪 GERMAN 🇮🇳 HINDI 🇨🇦 FRANÇAIS

BY Dr. BAK NGUYEN, Dr. PAUL OUELLETTE, Dr. PAUL DOMINIQUE, Dr. MARIA KUNSTADTER, Dr. EDWARD J. ZUCKERBERG, Dr. MASHA KHAGHANI, Dr. SUJATA BASAWARAJ, Dr. ALVA AURORA, Dr. JUDITH BÄUMLER, and Dr. ASHISH GUPTA

In ALPHA DENTISTRY, DIGITAL ORTHODONTICS FAQ, Dr. Bak is democratizing the science of dentistry, starting with orthodontics. In a word, he is sharing everything a patient needs to know on the matter in FAQ form, simple words you'll understand.10 International Alpha Doctors, from USA, Spain, Germany, India, and Canada are joining forces to make the knowledge complete and universal. ALPHA DENTISTRY is the first effort to create a universal knowledge in the field of dentistry, this is the orthodontics volume. This is the most ambitious book project in the History of Dentistry. ALPHA DENTISTRY is in response to the COVID crisis, the shortage of staff crisis, and the effort to unify dentistry to the Information Age, as discussed in RELEVANCY and COVIDCONOMICS, THE DENTAL INDUSTRY.

ALPHA LADDERS -075
CAPTAIN OF YOUR DESTINY
BY Dr. BAK NGUYEN & JONAS DIOP

In ALPHA LADDERS, Dr. Bak is sharing his private conversation and board meetings with 2 of his trusted lieutenants, strategist Jonas Diop and international Counsellor, Brenda Garcia. As both Dr. Bak and ALPHA brands are gaining in popularity and traction, it was time to get the movement to the next level. Now, it's about building a community and helping everyone willing to become ALPHAS to find their powers. Dr. Bak is a natural recruiter of ALPHAS and peers. He also spent the last 20 years plus, training and mentoring proteges. Now comes the time to empower more and more proteges to become ALPHAS. ALPHAS LADDERS is the journey of how Dr. Bak went from a product of Conformity to rise into a force of Nature, known as a kind tornado. In ALPHA LADDERS Jonas pushed Dr. Bak to retrace each of the steps of his awakening, steps that we can break down and reproduce for ourselves. The goal is to empower each willing individual to become the ultimate Captain of his or her destiny, and to do it, again and again. Welcome to the Alphas.

ALPHA LADDERS 2 -081
SHAPING LEADERS AND ACHIEVERS
BY Dr. BAK NGUYEN & BRENDA GARCIA

In ALPHA LADDERS 2, Dr. Bak is sharing the second part of his private conversation and board meetings with his trusted lieutenants. This time it is with international Counsellor, Brenda Garcia that the dialogue is taking place. In this second tome, the journey is taken to the next level. If the first tome was about the WHYs and the HOWs at an individual level, this tome is about the WHYs and the HOWs at the societal level. Through the lens of her background in international relations and diplomacy, Brenda now has the mission to help Dr. Bak establish structures, not only for his emerging organization and legacy, THE ALPHAS, but to also inspire all the other leaders and structures of our society. To do this, Brenda is taking Dr. Bak on an anthropological, sociological and philosophical journey to revisit different historical key moments in various fields and eras, going as far back as ancient Greece at the dawn of democracy, all the way to the golden era of modern multilateralism embodied by the UN structure. Learning from the legacies of prominent figures going from Plato to Ban Ki-Moon, Martin Luther King or Nelson Mandela, to Machiavelli, Marx and Simone de Beauvoir, Brenda and Dr. Bak are attempting to grasp the essence of structure and hierarchy, their goal being to empower each willing individual to become the ultimate Captain of their success, to climb up the ladders no matter how high it is, and to build their legacy one step at a time.

ALPHA MASTERMIND vol. 1 -116
THE SUPERHERO'S SYNDROME
BY Dr. BAK NGUYEN

ALPHA MASTERMIND, THE SUPER HERO'S SYNDROME, is not a superhero book, but it is the tale of every leader, entrepreneur, and everyday hero facing their destiny and entourage. It uncovers how society sees our best elements and expects from them. It covers how family and friends feel and why they act as they do. But most importantly, it covers how Alphas can emerge unscathed from their growth to uncover their true powers and purpose. A veteran agent of change and difference maker, Dr. Bak is sharing his experience and secret of why and how surfing through family and society pressure without revolting and without kneeling. THE SUPERHERO'S SYNDROME is the first volume inspired by the MASTERMINDS sessions as Dr. Bak is mentoring Alpha apprentices. The superhero's syndrome came to the table as Alphas are struggling to fit in society, to keep their values and generosity while facing so much negativity all around. Welcome to the Alphas.

AMONGST THE ALPHAS -058
BY Dr. BAK NGUYEN, with Dr. MARIA KUNSTADTER, Dr. PAUL OUELLETTE and Dr. JEREMY KRELL

In AMONGST THE ALPHAS, Dr. Bak opens the blueprint of the next level with the hope that everyone can be better, bigger, and wiser, but above all, a philosophy of Life that if, well applied, can bring inspiration to life. The Alphas rose in the midst of the COVID war as an International Collaboration to empower individuals to rise from the global crisis. Joining Dr. Bak are some of the world thinkers and achievers, the Alphas. Doctors, business people, thinkers, achievers, and influencers, are coming together to define what is an Alpha and his or her role, making the world a better place. This isn't the American dream, it is the human dream, one that can help you make History. Joining Dr. Bak are 3 Alpha authors, Dr. Maria Kunstadter, Dr. Paul Ouellette and Dr. Jeremy Krell. This book started with questions from coach Jonas Diop. Welcome to the Alphas.

AMONGST THE ALPHAS vol.2 -059
ON THE OTHER SIDE
BY Dr. BAK NGUYEN with Dr. JULIO REYNAFARJE, Dr. LINA DUSEVICIUTE and Dr. DUC-MINH LAM-DO

In AMONGST THE ALPHAS 2, Dr. Bak continues to explore the meaning of what it is to be an Alpha and how to act amongst Alphas, because as the saying taught us: alone one goes fast, together we go far. Some people see the problem. Some people look at the problem, some people created the problem. Some people leverage the problem into solutions and opportunities. Well, all of those people are Alphas. Networking and leveraging one another, their powers and reach are beyond measure. And one will keep the other in line too. Joining Dr. Bak are 3 Alphas from around the world coming together to share and collaborate, Dr. DUSEVICIUTE, Dr. LAM-DO and Dr. REYNAFARJE. This isn't the American dream, it is the human dream, one that can help you make History. Welcome to the Alphas.

AU PAYS DES PAPAS -106
BY Dr. BAK NGUYEN & WILLIAM BAK

On ne nait pas papa. On le devient. Dans sa quête d'être le meilleur papa possible pour William, Dr. Bak monte au pays des papas avec William à la recherche du papa parfait. Comme pour tout dans la vie, il doit exister une recette pour faire des papas parfaits. AU PAYS DES PAPAS est le récit des souvenirs des papas que Dr. Bak a croisé avant, alors et après qu'il soit devenu papa lui aussi. Une histoire drôle et innocente pour un Noël magique, ceci est la nouvelle aventure de William et de son papa, le Dr. Bak. Entre les livres de poulet, LEGENDS OF DESTINY et les des livres parentaux de Dr. Bak, AU PAYS DES PAPAS nous amène dans le monde magique de ces êtres magiques qui forgent des rêves, des vies et des destins.

AU PAYS DES PAPAS 2 -108
BY Dr. BAK NGUYEN & WILLIAM BAK

On ne nait pas papa, ça on le sait après le premier voyage AU PAYS DES PAPAS. Suite à leur première expédition, Dr. Bak et William ont compris qu'il n'y a pas de papas parfaits ni de recette pour faire des papas parfaits. Pourtant, les papas parfaits existent! Dans ce 2e récit AU PAYS DES PAPAS, William revient avec son papa, Dr. Bak, mais cette fois, c'est William qui dirige l'expédition. Même s'il n'existe pas de recette pour faire des papas parfaits, il doit toutefois exister des façons de rendre son papa meilleur, version 2.0! C'est la nouvelle quête de William et du Dr. Bak, à la recherche de la mise-à-jour parfaite pour le meilleur papa 2.0 possible! William est déterminé à tout pour trouver la recette cette fois-ci! AU PAYS DES PAPAS 2 est le nouveau récit des aventures père-fils du Dr. Bak et de William Bak, après AU PAYS DES PAPAS 1, les livres de poulets, LEGENDS OF DESTINY et les BOOKS OF LEGENDS.

B

BOOTCAMP -071
BOOKS TO REWRITE MINDSETS INTO WINNING STATES OF MIND
BY Dr. BAK NGUYEN

In BOOTCAMP 8 BOOKS TO REWRITE MINDSETS INTO WINNING STATES OF MIND, Dr. Bak is taking you into his past, before the visionary entrepreneur, before the world records, before the Industry's disruptor status. Here are 8 of the books that changed Dr. Bak's thinking and, therefore, reset his evolution into the course we now know him for. BOOTCAMP: 8 BOOKS TO REWRITE MINDSETS INTO WINNING STATES OF MIND, is a Bootcamp of 8 weeks for anyone looking to experience Dr. Bak's training to become THE Dr. BAK you came to know and love. This book will summarize how each title changed Dr. Bak's mindset into a state of mind and how he applied that to rewrite his destiny. 8 books to read, that's 8 weeks of Bootcamp to access the power of your MIND and your WILL. Are you ready for a change?

BRANDING -044
BALANCING STRATEGY AND EMOTIONS
BY Dr. BAK NGUYEN

BRANDING is communication to its most powerful state. Branding is not just about communicating anymore but about making a promise, about establishing a relationship, and about generating an emotion. More than once, Dr. Bak proved himself to be a master, communicating and branding his ideas into flags attracting interest and influence, nationally and internationally. In BRANDING, Dr. Bak shares a very unique and personal journey, branding Dr. Bak. How does he go from Dr. Nguyen, a loved and respected dentist to becoming Dr. Bak, a world anchor hosting THE ALPHAS in the medical and financial world? More than a personal journey, BRANDING helps to break down the steps to elevate someone with nothing else but the force of his or her spirit. Welcome to the Alphas.

C

CHANGING THE WORLD FROM A DENTAL CHAIR -007
BY Dr. BAK NGUYEN

Since he has received the EY's nomination for entrepreneur of the year for his startup Mdex & Co, Dr. Bak Nguyen has pushed the opportunity to the next level. Speaker, author, and businessman, Dr. Bak is a true entrepreneur and industries' disruptor. To compensate for the startup's status of Mdex & Co, he challenged himself to write a book based on the EY's questionnaire to share an in-depth vision of his company. With "Changing the World from a dental chair" Dr. Bak is sharing his thought process and philosophy to his approach to the industry. Not looking to revolutionize but rather to empower, he became, despite himself, an industries disruptor: an entrepreneur who has established a new benchmark. Dr. Bak Nguyen is a cosmetic dentist and visionary businessman who won the GRAND HOMAGE prize of "LYS de la Diversité" 2016, for his contribution as a citizen and entrepreneur in the community. He also holds recognitions from the Canadian Parliament and the Canadian Senate. In 2003, he founded Mdex, a dental company upon which in 2018, he launched the most ambitious private endeavour to reform the dental industry, Canada-wide. He wrote seven books covering ENTREPRENEURSHIP, LEADERSHIP, QUEST of IDENTITY, and now, PROFESSION HEALTH. Philosopher, he has close to his heart the quest of happiness of the people surrounding him, patients, and colleagues alike. Those projects have allowed Dr. Nguyen to attract interest from the international and diplomatic community and he is now the centre of a global discussion on the wellbeing and the future of the health profession. It is in that matter that he shares with you his thoughts and encourages the health community to share their own stories.

CHAMPION MINDSET -039
LEARNING TO WIN
BY Dr. BAK NGUYEN & CHRISTOPHE MULUMBA

CHAMPION MINDSET is the encounter of the business world and the professional sports world. Industries' Disruptor Dr. BAK NGUYEN shares his wisdom and views with the HAMMER, CFL Football Star, Edmonton's Eskimos CHRISTOPHE MULUMBA on how to leverage the champion mindset to create successful entrepreneurs. Writing and challenging each other, they discovered the parallels and the difference of both worlds, but mainly, the recipe for leveraging from one to succeed in the other, from champions and entrepreneurs to WINNERS. Build and score your millions, it is a matter of mindset! This is CHAMPION MINDSET.

COMMENT ÉCRIRE UN LIVRE EN 30 JOURS -102
PAR Dr. BAK NGUYEN

Dans COMMENT ÉCRIRE UN LIVRE EN 30 JOURS, après plus de 100 livres écrits en 4 ans, le Dr Bak revisite son premier succès, le livre dans lequel il a partagé son art et sa structure d'écriture de livres. Encore et encore, le Dr Bak a prouvé que non seulement le contenu est important, mais ce sont la structure et le processus qui rendent les livres. L'inspiration n'est que le début. Si vous envisagez d'écrire votre premier livre, ceci est votre chance. Si vous y pensez, faites-le, et aussi vite que possible. Écrire votre premier livre vous libérera de votre passé et vous ouvrira les portes de votre avenir! Tout le monde a une histoire qui mérite d'être partagée! Par où commencer, comment passer le MUR DE L'INSPIRATION, quelles sont les techniques pour apporter de la profondeur à votre histoire, comment structurer votre chapitre, combien de chapitres, comment avoir un livre, en un mois? Voilà les réponses que vous trouverez dans COMMENT ÉCRIRE UN LIVRE EN 30 JOURS. Vous trouverez un trésor de sagesse, un mentor et surtout, une confiance renouvelée pour écrire, que ce soit, votre premier, deuxième ou même 10e livre. Au fait, le Dr. Bak a écrit ce livre et l'a fait publier en 6 jours. Bienvenu(e)s aux Alphas.

COMMENT ÉCRIRE 2 LIVRES EN 10 JOURS -115
Par WILLIAM & Dr. BAK NGUYEN

Dans COMMENT ÉCRIRE 2 LIVRES EN 10 JOURS, William Bak s'attaque au succès de son père, COMMENT ÉCRIRE UN LIVRE EN 30 JOURS. Cette fois-ci, père et fils font équipe pour vous partager l'art d'écrire de la fiction. Comme le titre le mentionne, William doit écrire ce livre et le suivant en 10 jours. Pour ne pas vous induire en erreur, écrire votre premier livre de fiction prendra plus que 10 jours. Cependant, les procédés contenus dans ce livre vous aideront à accélérer votre production et à porter votre créativité à des niveaux inégalés. William a 12 ans et déjà, il a signé 36 livres dont la plupart sont de la fiction. En ce sens, il est un vétéran auteur, un qui a connu les hauts et les bas du manque d'inspiration. Au côté de William, Dr. Bak se prête aussi au jeux de démolir son propre succès et le remplacer par une nouvelle marque. Père et fils, ils vous partagent leurs secrets et expérience à écrire un duo-choque depuis les derniers 4 ans. COMMENT ÉCRIRE 2 LIVRES EN 10 JOURS a commencé par une farce qui est rapidement devenu leur plus grand défi à ce jour, d'écrire 2 livres en 10 jours. Bienvenu(e)s aux Alphas.

COVIDCONOMIE -111
CONTRER L'INFLATION SANS TOUCHER LES TAUX D'INTÉRÊT
PAR Dr. BAK NGUYEN, ANDRÉ CHÂTEALAIN, TRANIE VO, FRANÇOIS DUFOUR, WILLIAM BAK

COVIDCONOMIE est l'ensemble des observations, analyses des phénomènes démographiques et économiques secondaires à la pandémie de la COVID-19. CONTRER L'INFLATION SANS TOUCHER LES TAUX D'INTÉRÊT, est la réflexion et plan macro des ALPHAS pour le CANADA et les ÉTATS-UNIS D'AMÉRIQUE dans un premier temps et un modèle économique pour l'ensemble des pays d'Occident.Joint par des leaders en finance et en économie, dont André Châtelain, ancien premier vice-président du MOUVEMENT DESJARDINS, le Dr. Bak met la table à des discussions inclusives et constructives pouvant changer le cours de l'Histoire dans l'intérêt des citoyens au quotidien.CONTRER L'INFLATION SANS TOUCHER LES TAUX D'INTÉRÊT, est un mémoire collectif des

ALPHAS pour lutter contre l'inflation post-pandémique et éviter une récession internationale globale.

COVIDCONOMICS -112
TAMING INFLATION WITHOUT INCREASING INTEREST RATES
BY Dr. BAK NGUYEN, ANDRÉ CHÂTEALAIN, TRANIE VO, FRANÇOIS DUFOUR, WILLIAM BAK

COVIDCONOMICS, are the reflections, analysis and discussion of the ALPHAS, hosted by Dr. Bak to understand the demographic et economical trends post-COVID-19. TAMING INFLATION WITHOUT INCREASING INTEREST RATES is a macro plan by the ALPHAS for Canada and the USA which can inspire a new economical model for all of the Western worlds. Joined by leaders in finance as André Châtelain, former 1st Vice-President of the MOUVEMENT DESJARDINS, Dr. Bak is hosting an inclusive discussion to save our economy in these very troubled times as the country is still looking to get back on its feet from the Pandemic while wars are raging on multiple fronts. TAMING INFLATION WITHOUT INCREASING INTEREST RATES is our proposal to save the economy and our recovery from a global recession.

E

EMPOWERMENT -069
BY Dr. BAK NGUYEN

In EMPOWERMENT, Dr. Bak's 69th book, writing a book every 8 days for 8 weeks in a row to write the next world record of writing 72 books/36 months, Dr. Bak is taking a rest, sharing his inner feelings, inspiration, and motivation. Much more than his dairy, EMPOWERMENT is the key to walking in his footsteps and comprehending the process of an overachiever. Dr. Bak's helped and inspired countless people to find their voice, to live their dream, and to be the better version of themselves. Why is he sharing as much and keep sharing? Why is he going that fast, always further and further, why and how is he keeping his inspiration and momentum? Those are all the answers EMPOWERMENT will deliver to you. This book might be one of the fastest Dr. Bak has written, not because of time constraints but from inspiration, pure inspiration to share and to grow. There is always a dark side to each power, two faces to a coin. Well, this is the less prominent facet of Dr. Bak's Momentum and success, the road to his MINDSET.

F

FORCES OF NATURE -015
FORGING THE CHARACTER OF WINNERS
BY Dr. BAK NGUYEN

In FORCES OF NATURE, Dr. Bak is giving his all. This is his 15 books written within 15 months. It is the end of a marathon to set the next world record. For the occasion, he wanted to end with a big bang! How about a book with all of his biggest challenges? In a Quest of Identity, a journey looking for his name and powers, Dr. Bak is borrowing myths and legends to make this journey universal. Yes, this is Dr. Bak's mythology. Demons, heroes and Gods, there are forces of Nature that we all meet on our way for our name. Some will scare us, some will fight us, and some will manipulate us. We can flee, we can hide, we can fight. What we do will define our next encounter and the one after. A tale of personal growth, a journey to find power and purpose, Dr. Bak is showing us the path to freedom, the Path of Life. Welcome to the Alphas.

H

HORIZON, BUILDING UP THE VISION -045
VOLUME ONE
BY Dr. BAK NGUYEN

Dr. Bak is opening up to your demand! Many of you are following Dr. Bak online and are asking to know more about his lifestyle. This is how he has chosen to respond: sharing his lifestyle as he travelled the world and what he learnt in each city to come to build his Mindset as a driver and a winner. Here are 10 destinations (over 69 that will be followed in the next volumes...) in which he shares his journey. New York, Quebec, Paris, Punta Cana, Monaco, Los Angeles, Nice, and Holguin, the journey happened over twenty years.

HORIZON, ON THE FOOTSTEP OF TITANS -048
VOLUME TWO
BY Dr. BAK NGUYEN

Dr. Bak is opening up to your demand! Many of you are following Dr. Bak online and are asking to know more about his lifestyle. This is how he has chosen to respond: sharing his lifestyle as he travelled the world and what he learnt in each city to come to build his Mindset as a driver and a winner. Here are 9 destinations (over 72 that will follow in the next volumes...) in which he shares his journey. Hong Kong, London, Rome, San Francisco, Anaheim, and more..., the journey happened over twenty years. Dr. Bak is sharing with you his feelings, impressions, and how they shaped his state of mind and character into Dr. Bak. From a dreamer to a driver and a builder, the journey started when he was 3. Wealth is a state of mind, and a state of mind is the basis of the drive. Find out about the mind of an Industry's disruptor.

HORIZON, DREAMING OF THE FUTURE -068
VOLUME THREE
BY Dr. BAK NGUYEN

Dr. Bak is back. From the midst of confinement, he remembers and writes about what life was, when travelling was a natural part of Life. It will come back. Now more than ever, we need to open both our hearts and minds to fight fear and intolerance. Writing from a time of crisis, he is sharing the magic and psychological effect of seeing the world and how it has shaped his mindset. Here are 9 other destinations (over 75) in which he shares his journey. Beijing, Key West, Madrid, Amsterdam, Marrakech and more…, the journey happened over twenty years.

HOW TO TO BOOST YOUR CREATIVITY TO NEW HEIGHTS -088
BY Dr. BAK NGUYEN

In HOW TO BOOST YOUR CREATIVITY TO NEW HEIGHTS, Dr. Bak is sharing his secrets of creativity and insane production pace with the world. Up to lately, Dr. Bak shared his secrets about speed and momentum but never has he opened up about where he gets his inspiration, time and time again. To celebrate his new world record of writing 100 books in 4 years, Dr. Bak is joined by his proteges strategist Jonas Diop, international counsellor Brenda Garcia and prodigy William Bak for the writing of his secrets on creativity. Brenda, Jonas and William all have witnessed Dr. Bak's creativity. This time, they will stand in to ask the right questions to unleash that creative power in ways for others to follow the trail. Part of the MILLION DOLLAR MINDSET series, HOW TO BOOST YOUR CREATIVITY TO NEW HEIGHTS is Dr. Bak's open book to one of his superpowers.

HOW TO NOT FAIL AS A DENTIST -047
BY Dr. BAK NGUYEN

In HOW TO NOT FAIL AS A DENTIST, Dr. Bak is given 20 plus years of experience and knowledge of what it is to be a dentist on the ground. PROFESSIONAL INTELLIGENCE, FINANCIAL INTELLIGENCE and MANAGEMENT INTELLIGENCE are the fields that any dentist will have to master for a chance to succeed and a shot at happiness, practicing dentistry. Where ever you are starting your career as a new graduate or a veteran in the field looking to reach the next level, this is book smart and street smart all into one. This is Million Dollar Mindset applied to dentistry. We won't be making a millionaire out of you from this book, we will be giving you a shot at happiness and success. The million will follow soon enough.

HOW TO WRITE A BOOK IN 30 DAYS -042
BY Dr. BAK NGUYEN

In HOW TO WRITE A BOOK IN 30 DAYS, after more than 100 books written in 4 years, Dr. Bak is revisiting his first hit, the book in which he shared his craft and structure of how to write books. After 100 books, Dr. Bak proved that not only content is important, but what will keep the words coming are the structure and the process. If you are looking into writing your first book, this is your chance. If you are thinking about it, do it, and as fast as possible. Writing your first book will set you free from your past and open the doors to your own future! Everyone has a story worth telling! Where to start, how to get by the INSPIRATIONAL WALL, what are the techniques to bring depth into your storytelling, how to structure your chapter, how many chapters, how to have a book, in a month? These are the answers you will find within HOW TO WRITE A BOOK IN 30 DAYS. You will find a wealth of wisdom from his experience writing your first, second or even 10th book. Dr. Bak is sharing his secrets writing books. By the way, he wrote this book and got it published within 6 days. Welcome to the Alphas.

HOW 2 WRITE 2 BOOKS IN 10 DAYS -114
BY WILLIAM & Dr. BAK NGUYEN

HOW 2 WRITE 2 BOOKS IN 10 DAYS, is William Bak takes on his father's hit, HOW TO WRITE A BOOK IN 30 DAYS. This time, William is covering the art of writing fiction. As mentioned in the title, William is writing this book and the next one within 10 days. Just not to mislead you, writing fiction will take longer, but once you have done all your prep work and research, it can be written as quickly. William is only 12 and already, he has signed 35 books. Most of his books are fiction, so on the matter, he is a veteran author, one with much experience of the ups and downs when it comes to writing books and getting them to the finish line Joining him is Dr. Bak who is sharing his secrets of writing fiction too. What does it take, how different it is from writing non-fictional books and what does it take to inspire and motivate his 12-year-old son to write as much, matching his world record pace? HOW 2 WRITE 2 BOOKS IN 10 DAYS is a joke between 2 world record authors teasing one another as they keep raising the bar higher and higher. Welcome to the Alphas.

HOW TO WRITE A SUCCESSFUL BUSINESS PLAN -049
BY Dr. BAK NGUYEN & ROUBA SAKR

In HOW TO WRITE A SUCCESSFUL BUSINESS PLAN, Dr. Bak is given 20 plus years of experience and knowledge of what it is to be an entrepreneur and more importantly, how to have the investors and banks on your side. Being an entrepreneur is surely not something you learn from school, but there are steps to master so you can communicate your views and vision. That's the only way you will have financing. Writing a business is only not a mandatory stop only for the bankers, but an essential step for every entrepreneur, to know the direction and what's coming next. A business plan is also not set in stone, if there is a truth in business is that nothing will go as planned. Writing down your business plan the first time will prepare you to adapt and overcome the challenges and surprises. For most entrepreneurs, a business is a passion. To most investors and all banks, a business is a system. Your business plan is the map to that system. However unique your ideas and business are, the mapping follows the same steps and pattern.

HUMILITY FOR SUCCESS -051
BALANCING STRATEGY AND EMOTIONS
BY Dr. BAK NGUYEN

HUMILITY FOR SUCCESS is exploring the emotional discomforts and challenges champions, and overachievers put themselves through. Success is never done overnight and on the way, just like the pain and the struggles aren't enough, we are dealing with the doubts, the haters, and those who like to tell us how to live our lives and what to do. At the same time, nothing of worth can be achieved alone. Every legend has a cast of characters, allies, mentors, companions, rivals, and foes. So one needs the key to social behaviour. HUMILITY FOR SUCCESS is exploring the matter and will help you sort out beliefs from values, and peers from friends. Humility is much more about how we see ourselves than how others see us. For any entrepreneur and champion, our daily is to set our mindset right, and to perfect our skills, not to fit in. There is a world where CONFIDENCE grows in synergy with HUMILITY. As you set the right label on the right belief, you will be able to grow and leave the lies and haters far behind. This is HUMILITY FOR SUCCESS.

HYBRID -011
THE MODERN QUEST OF IDENTITY
BY Dr. BAK NGUYEN

I

IDENTITY -004
THE ANTHOLOGY OF QUESTS
BY Dr. BAK NGUYEN

What if John Lennon was still alive and running for president today? What kind of campaign will he be running? IDENTIFY -THE ANTHOLOGY OF QUESTS is about the quest each of us has to undertake, sooner or later, THE QUEST OF IDENTITY. Citizens of the world, aim to be one, the one, one whole, one unity, made of many. That's the anthology of life! Start with your one, find your unity, and your legend will start. We are all small-minded people anyway! We need each other to be one! We need each other to be happy, so we, so you, so I, can be happy. This is the chorus of life. This is our song! Citizens of the world, I salute you! This is the first tome of the IDENTITY QUEST. FORCES OF NATURE (tome 2) will be following in SUMMER 2021. Also under development, Tome 3 - THE CONQUEROR WITHIN will start production soon.

INDUSTRIES DISRUPTORS -006
BY Dr. BAK NGUYEN

INDUSTRIES DISRUPTORS   is a strange title, one that sparkles mixed feelings. A disruptor is someone making a difference, and since we, in general, do not like change, the label is mostly negative. But a disruptor is mostly someone who sees the same problem and challenge from another angle. The disruptor will tackle that angle and come up with something new from something existent. That's evolution! In INDUSTRIES DISRUPTORS, Dr. Bak is joining forces with James Stephan-Usypchuk to share with us what is going on in the minds and shoes of those entrepreneurs disrupting the old habits. Dr. Bak is changing the world from a dental chair, disrupting the dental, and now the book industry. James is a maverick in the Intelligence space, from marketing to Artificial Intelligence. Coming from very different backgrounds and industries, they end up telling very similar stories. If disruptors change the world, well, their story proves that disruptors can be made and forged. Here's the recipe. Here are their stories.

K

KRYPTO -040
TO SAVE THE WORLD
BY Dr. BAK NGUYEN & ILYAS BAKOUCH

L

L'ART DE TRANSFORMER DE LA SOUPE EN MAGIE -103
PAR Dr. BAK NGUYEN

Dans L'ART DE TRANSFORMER DE LA SOUPE EN MAGIE, Dr. Bak remonte aux sources pour connaître la source de son génie et la recette qui a été transféré à son fils, William Bak, auteur et record mondial dès l'âge de 8 ans. Docteur en médecine dentaire, entrepreneur, écrivain record mondial, musicien, Dr. Bak est d'abord et avant tout un fils qui a une maman qui croit en lui. L'ART DE TRANSFORMER DE LA SOUPE EN MAGIE est dédié à la recette du génie, celle qui pousse une mère a mijoté les ingrédients de l'espoir dans un bouillon d'amour, à y ajuster un zeste de bonheur et un brin d'ambition. Dans la lignée des livres parentaux de Dr. Bak, L'ART DE TRANSFORMER DE LA

SOUPE EN MAGIE est dédié à la première femme dans sa vie, celle qui a tracé son destin et celle qui l'a cultivée.

LEADERSHIP -003
PANDORA'S BOX
BY Dr. BAK NGUYEN

LEADERSHIP, PANDORA'S BOX is 21 presidential speeches for a better tomorrow for all of us. It aims to drive HOPE and motivation into each and every one of us. Together we can make the difference, we hold such power. Covering themes from LOYALTY to GENEROSITY, from FREEDOM and INTELLIGENCE to DOUBTS and DEATH, this is not the typical presidential or motivational speeches that we are used to. LEADERSHIP PANDORA'S BOX will surf your emotions first, only to dive with you to touch the core and soul of our meaning: to matter. This is not a Quest of Identity, but the cry to rally as a species, raise our heads toward the future and move forward as a WHOLE. Not a typical Dr. Bak's book, LEADERSHIP, PANDORA'S BOX is a must-read for all of you looking for hope and purpose, all of us, citizens of the world.

LEVERAGE -014
COMMUNICATION INTO SUCCESS
BY Dr. BAK NGUYEN

In LEVERAGE COMMUNICATION TO SUCCESS, Dr. Bak shares his secret and mindsets to elevate an idea into a vision and a vision into an endeavour. Some endeavours will be a project, some others will become companies, and some will grow into a movement. It does not matter, each started with great communication. Communication is a very vast concept, education, sale, sharing, empowering, coaching, preaching, and entertaining. Those are all different kinds of communication. The intent differs, the audiences vary, and the messages are unique but the frame can be templated and mastered. In LEVERAGE COMMUNICATION TO SUCCESS, Dr. Bak is loyal to his core, sharing only what he knows best, what he has done himself. This book is dedicated to communicating successfully in business.

LEGENDS OF DESTINY vol.1 -101
THE PROLOGUES OF DESTINY
BY Dr. BAK NGUYEN & WILLIAM BAK

The war between the forces of death and the legions of life lasted for centuries, ravaging most of the twin planets, Destiny and Earth. The end was so imminent that even the Gods got involved to save Life from eternal doom. Heroes rise and fall from all sides. Some fight for good, others, for evil. Gods, titans, angels, and demons all took sides in the war. Gods fight and kill other gods. Angel fights alongside demons, striking down Gods and Titans, and rival angels. The war lasted for so long that no one even remembers what they were fighting for. Some fight for domination while others, just to survive. The war ravages Destiny, the twin sister of planet Earth to the brink of annihilation. All eyes now turn to Earth. As the balance of the creation itself hands in the balance, a species emerges as holding the balance to victory: mankind. For the future of Humanity, of Gods and men and everything in between, this is the last stand of Destiny, a last chance for life.

LEGENDS OF DESTINY vol.2
THE BOOK OF ELVES
BY Dr. BAK NGUYEN & WILLIAM BAK

Caught between the Orcs invading from the center of Destiny, the Angels raining down and the Demons eating from within, the Elves are turning from their old beliefs and Gods for salvation. For Millennials, Elves turned to Odin and the Forces of Nature for answers and guidance. Since the imminent destruction of their kingdoms and cities, a new God is offering Hope, Kal, the old God of fire. Kal gave them more than Hope, he gave the elves who turned to him for passage to a new world. But more than hope, more than fear, Elves value honour and Destiny. At least their old guards and heroes do. With their world crumbling down, and the rise of the new and younger generations, Elf's society seems to be at the crossroad of evolution. It is convert or die. Or die fighting or die kneeling. The Book of Elves is the story of a civilization facing its fate in the blink of destruction.

M

MASTERMIND, 7 WAYS INTO THE BIG LEAGUE
BY Dr. BAK NGUYEN & JONAS DIOP

MASTERMIND, 7 WAYS INTO THE BIG LEAGUE is the result of the encounter between business coach Jonas Diop and Dr. Bak. As a professional podcaster and someone always seeking the truth and ways to leverage success and performance, coach Jonas is putting Dr. Bak to the test, one that should reveal his secret to overachieve month after month, accumulating a new world record every month. Follow those two great minds as they push each other to surpass themselves, each in their own way and own style. MASTERMIND, 7 WAYS INTO THE BIG LEAGUE is more than a roadmap to success, it is a journey and a live testimony as you are turning the pages, one by one.

MIDAS TOUCH -065
POST-COVID DENTISTRY
BY Dr. BAK NGUYEN, Dr. JULIO REYNAFARJE AND Dr. PAUL OUELLETTE

MIDAS TOUCH, is the memoir of what happened in the ALPHAS SUMMIT in the midst of the GREAT PAUSE as great minds throughout the world in the dental field are coming together. As the time of competition is obsolete, the new era of collaboration is blooming. This is the 3rd book of the ALPHAS, after AFTERMATH and RELEVANCY, all written in the midst of confinement. Dr. Julio Reynafarje is bearing this initiative, to share with you the secret of a successful and lasting relationship with your patients, balancing science and psychology, kindness, and professionalism. He personally invited the ALPHAS to join as co-author, Dr. Paul Ouellette, Dr. Paul Dominique, and Dr. Bak. Together, they have more than 100 years of combined experience, wisdom, trade, skills, philosophy, and secrets to share with you to empower you in the rebuilding of the dental profession in the aftermath of COVID. RELEVANCY was about coming together and rebuilding the future. MIDAS TOUCH is about how to build, one treatment plan at a time, one story at a time, one smile at a time.

MINDSET ARMORY -050
BY Dr. BAK NGUYEN

MINDSET ARMORY is Dr. Bak's 49th book, days after he completed his world record of writing 48 books within 24 months, on top of being the CEO of Mdex & Co and a full-time cosmetic dentist. Dr. Bak is undoubtedly an OVERACHIEVER. In his last books, he has shared more and more of his lifestyle and how it forged his winning mindset. Within MINDSET ARMORY, Dr. Bak is sharing with us his tools, how he found them, forged them, and leverage them. Just like any warrior needs a shield, a sword, and a ride, here are Dr. Bak's. For any entrepreneur, the road to success is a long and winding journey. On the way, some will find allies and foes. Some allies will become foes, and some foes might become allies. In today's competitive world, the only constant is change. With the right tool, it is possible to achieve. The right tool, the right mindset. This is MINDSET ARMORY.

MIRROR -085
BY Dr. BAK NGUYEN

MIRROR is the theme for a personal book. Not only to Dr. Bak but to all of us looking to reach beyond who and what we actually are. MIRROR is special in the fact that it is not only the content of the book that is of worth but the process in which Dr. Bak shared his own evolution. To go beyond who we are, one must grow every day. And how do you compare your growth and how far have you reached? Looking in the mirror. In all of Dr. Bak's writing, looking at the past is a trap to avoid at all costs. Looking in the mirror, is that any better? Share Dr. Bak's way to push and keep pushing himself without friction or resistance. Please read that again. To evolve without friction or resistance… that is the source of infinite growth and the unification of the Quest for Power and the Quest of Happiness.

MOMENTUM TRANSFER -009
BY Dr. BAK NGUYEN & Coach DINO MASSON

How to be successful in your business and life? Achieve Your Biggest Goals With MOMENTUM TRANSFER. START THE BUSINESS YOU WANT - AND BRING IT NEXT LEVEL! GET THE LIFE YOU ALWAYS WANTED - AND IMPROVE IT! TAKE ANY PROJECTS YOU HAVE - AND MAKE THEM THE BEST! In this powerful book, you'll discover what a small business owner learnt from a millionaire and successful entrepreneur. He applied his mentor's principles and is explaining them in full detail in this book. The small business owner wrote the book he has always wanted to read and went from the verge of bankruptcy to quadrupling his revenues in less than 9 months and improve his personal life by increasing his energy and bringing back peacefulness. Together, the millionaire and the small business owner are sharing their most valuable business and life lessons with the world. The most powerful book to increase your momentum in your business and your life introduces simple and radical life-changing concepts: Multiply your business revenues by finding the Eye of your Momentum - Increase your energy by building and feeding your own Momentum - How to increase your confidence with these simple steps - How to transfer your new powerful energy into other aspects of your business and life - How to set goals and achieve them (even crush them!)- How to always tap into an effortless and limitless force within you- And much, much more!

P

PLAYBOOK INTRODUCTION -055
BY Dr. BAK NGUYEN

In PLAYBOOK INTRODUCTION, Dr. Bak is open the door to all the newcomers and aspirant entrepreneurs who are looking at where and when to start. Based on questions of two college students wanting to know how to start their entrepreneurial journey, Dr. Bak dives into his experiences to empower the next generation, not about what they should do, but how he, Dr. Bak, would have done it today. This is an important aspect to recognize in the business world, the world has changed since the INFORMATION AGE and the advent of the millenniums into the market. Most matrix and know-how have to be adapted to today's speed and accessibility to the information. We are living at the INFORMATION AGE, this book is the precursor to the ABUNDANCE AGE, at least to those open to embracing the opportunity.

PLAYBOOK INTRODUCTION 2 -056
BY Dr. BAK NGUYEN

In PLAYBOOK INTRODUCTION 2, Dr. Bak continues the journey to welcome the newcomers and aspirant entrepreneurs looking at where and when to start. If the first volume covers the mindset, the second is covering much more in-depth the concept of debt and leverage. This is an important aspect to recognize in the business world, the world has changed since the INFORMATION AGE and the advent of the millenniums into the market. Most matrix and know-how have to be adapted to today's speed and accessibility to the information. We are living at the INFORMATION AGE, this book is the precursor to the ABUNDANCE AGE, at least to those open to embrace the opportunity.

POWER -043
EMOTIONAL INTELLIGENCE
BY Dr. BAK NGUYEN

IN POWER, EMOTIONAL INTELLIGENCE, Dr. Bak is sharing his experiences and secrets leveraging on his EMOTIONAL INTELLIGENCE, a power we all have within. From SYMPATHY, having others opening up to you, to ACTIVE LISTENING, saving you time and energy; from EMPATHY, allowing you to predict the future to INFLUENCE, enabling you to draft the future, not to forget the power of the crowd with MOMENTUM, you are now in possession of power in tune with nature, yourself. It is a unique take on the subject to empower you to find your powers and your destiny. Visionary businessman, and doctor in dentistry, Dr. Bak describes himself as a Dentist by circumstances, a communicator by passion, and an entrepreneur by nature.

POWERPLAY -078
HOW TO BUILD THE PERFECT TEAM
BY Dr. BAK NGUYEN

In POWERPLAY, HOW TO BUILD THE PERFECT TEAM, Dr. Bak is sharing with you his experience, perspective, and mistake travelling the journey of the entrepreneur. A serial entrepreneur himself, he started venture only with a single partner as a team to build companies with a director of human resources and a board of directors. POWERPLAY is not a story, it is the HOW TO build the perfect team, knowing that perfection is a lie. So how can one build a team that will empower his or her vision? How to recruit, how to train, how to retain? Those are all legitimate questions. And all of those won't matter if the first question isn't answered: what is the reason for the team? There is the old way to hire and the new way to recruit. Yes, Human Resources is all about mindset too! This journey is one of introspection, of leadership, and a cheat sheet to build, not only the perfect team but the team that will empower your legacy to the next level.

PROFESSION HEALTH - TOME ONE -005
THE UNCONVENTIONAL QUEST OF HAPPINESS
BY Dr. BAK NGUYEN, Dr. MIRJANA SINDOLIC, Dr. ROBERT DURAND AND COLLABORATORS

Why are health professionals burning out while they give the best of themselves to heal the world? Dr. Bak aims to break the curse of isolation that health professionals face and establish a conversation to start the healing process. PROFESSION HEALTH is the basis of an ongoing discussion and will also serve as an introduction to a study led by Professor Robert Durand, DMD, MSc Science from the University of Montreal, a study co-financed by Mdex and the Federal Government of Canada. Co-writers are Dr. Mirjana Sindolic, Professor Robert Durand, Dr. Jean De Serres, MD and former President of Hema Quebec, Counsel-Minister Luis Maria Kalaff Sanchez, Dr. Miguel Angel Russo, MD, Banker Anthony Siggia, Banker Kyles Yves, and more... This is the first Tome of three, dedicated to helping "WHITE COATS" to heal and to find their happiness.

R

REBOOT -012
MIDLIFE CRISIS
BY Dr. BAK NGUYEN

MidLife Crisis is a common theme for each of us as we reach the threshold. As a man, as a woman, why is it that half of the marriages end up in recall? If anything else would have half those rates of failure, the lawsuits would be raining. Where are the flaws, the traps? Love is strong and pure, why is marriage not the reflection of that? Those are all hard questions to ask with little or no answers. Dr. Bak is sharing his reflections and findings as he reached himself the WALL OF MARRIAGE. This is a matter that affects all of our lives. It is time for some answers.

RELEVANCY - TOME TWO -064
REINVENTING OURSELVES TO SURVIVE
BY Dr. BAK NGUYEN & Dr. PAUL OUELLETTE AND COLLABORATORS

THE GREAT PAUSE was a reboot of all the systems of society. Many outdated systems will not make it back. The Dental Industry is a needed one, it has laid on complacency for far too long. In an age where expertise is global and democratized and can be replaced with technologies and artificial intelligence, the REBOOT will force, not just an update, but an operating system replacement and a firmware upgrade. First, they saved their industry with THE ALPHAS INITIATIVE, sharing their knowledge and vision freely to all the world's dental industry. With the OUELLETTE INITIATIVE, they bought some time for all the dental clinics to resume and adjust. The warning has been given, the clock is now ticking. who will prevail and prosper and who will be left behind, outdated and obsolete?

RISING -062
TO WIN MORE THAN YOU ARE AFRAID TO LOSE
BY Dr. BAK NGUYEN

In RISING, TO WIN MORE TAN YOU ARE AFRAID TO LOSE, Dr. Bak is breaking down the strategy to success to all, not only those wearing white coats and scrubs. More than his previous book (SUCCESS IS A CHOICE), this one is covering most of the aspects of getting to the next level, psychologically, socially, and financially. Rising is broken down into three key strategies: Financial Leverage - Compressing time - Always being in control. Presented by MILLION DOLLAR MINDSET, the book is covering more than the ways to create wealth, but also how to reach happiness and live a life without regrets. Dr. Bak the CEO and founder of Mdex & Co, a company with the promise of reforming the whole dental industry for the better. He wrote more than 60 books within 30 months as he is sharing his experiences, secrets, and wisdom.

S

SELFMADE -036
GRATITUDE AND HUMILITY
BY Dr. BAK NGUYEN

This is the story of Dr. Bak, an artist who became a dentist, a dentist who became an Entrepreneur, an Entrepreneur who is seeking to save an entire industry. In his free time, Dr. Bak managed to write 37 books and is a contender for 3 world records to be confirmed. Businessman and visionary, his views and philosophy are ahead of our time. This is his 37th book. In SELFMADE, Dr. Bak is answering the questions most entrepreneurs want to know, the HOWTO and the secret recipes, not just to succeed, but to keep going no matter what! SELFMADE is the perfect read for any entrepreneurs, novices, and veterans.

SHORTCUT vol. 1 - HEALING -093
BY Dr. BAK NGUYEN

In SHORTCUT 408 HEALING QUOTES, Dr. Bak revisits and compiles his journey of healing and growing. Just like anyone, he was moulded and shaped by Conformity and Society to the point of blending and melting. Walking his journey of healing, he rediscovers himself and found his true calling. And once whole with himself and with the Universe, Dr. Bak found his powers. In SHORTCUT 408 HEALING QUOTES, you have a quick and easy way to surf his mindsets and what allowed him to heal, to find back his voice and wings, and to walk his destiny. You too are walking your Quest of Identity. That one is mainly a journey of healing. May you find yours and your powers.

SHORTCUT vol. 2 - GROWING -094
BY Dr. BAK NGUYEN

In SHORTCUT 408 GROWTH QUOTES, Dr. Bak is compiling his library of books about personal growth and self-improvement. More than a motivational book, more than a compilation of knowledge, Dr. Bak is sharing the mindsets upon which he found his power to achieve and to overachieve. We all have our powers, only they were muted and forgotten as we were forged by Conformity and Society. After the healing process, walking your Quest of Identity, the Quest for your growth and God-given power is next to lead you to walk your Destiny.

SHORTCUT vol. 3 - LEADERSHIP -095
BY Dr. BAK NGUYEN

In SHORTCUT 365 LEADERSHIP QUOTES, Dr. Bak is compiling his library of books about leadership and ambition. Yes, the ambition is to find your worth and to make the world a better place for all of us. If the 3rd volume of SHORTCUT is mainly a motivational compilation, it also holds the secrets and mindsets to influence and leadership. If you were looking to walk your legend and impact the world, you are walking a lonely path. You might on your own, but it does not have to be harder than it is. As we all have your unique challenges, the key to victory is often found in the same place, your heart. And here are 365 shortcuts to keep you believing and to attract more people to you as you are growing into a true leader.

SHORTCUT vol. 4 - CONFIDENCE -096
BY Dr. BAK NGUYEN

SHORTCUT 518 CONFIDENCE QUOTES, is the most voluminous compilation of Dr. Bak's quotes. To heal was the first step. To grow and find your powers came next. As you are walking your personal legend, Confidence is both your sword and armour to conquer your Destiny and overcome all of the challenges on your way. In SHORTCUT volume four, Dr. Bak comprises all his mindsets and wisdom to ease your ascension. Confidence is not something one is simply born with, but something to nurture, grow, and master. Some will have the chance to be raised by people empowering Confidence, others will have to heal from Conformity to grow their confidence. It does not matter, only once Confident, can one stand tall and see clearly the horizon.

SHORTCUT vol. 5- SUCCESS -097
BY Dr. BAK NGUYEN

Success is not a destination but a journey and a side effect. While no map can lead you to success, the right mindset will forge your own success, the one without medals nor labels. If you are looking to walk your legend, to be successful is merely the beginning. Actually, being successful is often a side effect of the mindsets and actions that you took, you provoked. In SHORTCUT 317 SUCCESS QUOTES, Dr. Bak is revisiting his journey, breaking down what led him to be successful despite the odds stacked against him. As success is the consequence of mindsets, choices, and actions, it can be duplicated over and over again, one just needs to master the mindsets first.

SHORTCUT vol. 6- POWER -098
BY Dr. BAK NGUYEN

That's the kind of power that you will discover within this journey. Power is a tool, a leverage. Well used, it will lead to great achievements. Misused, it will be your downfall. If a sword sometimes has 2 edges, Power is a sword with no handle and multiple edges. You have been warned. In SHORTCUT 376 POWER QUOTES, Dr. Bak is compiling all the powers he found and mastered walking his own legend. If the first power was Confidence, very quickly, Dr. Bak realized that Confidence was the key to many, many more powers. Where to find them, how to yield them, and how to leverage these powers is the essence of the 6th volume of SHORTCUT.

SHORTCUT vol. 7- HAPPINESS -099
BY Dr. BAK NGUYEN

We were all born happy and then, somehow, we lost our ways and forgot our ways home. Is this the real tragedy behind the lost paradise myth? If we were happy once, we can trust our hearts to find our way home, once more. This is the journey of the 7th volume of the SHORTCUT series. In SHORTCUT 306 HAPPINESS QUOTES, Dr. Bak is revisiting and compiling all the secrets and mindsets leading to happiness. Happiness is not just a destination but a shrine for Confidence and a safe place to regroup, to heal, to grow. We each have our own happiness. What you will learn here is where to find yours and, more importantly, how to leverage you to ease the journey ahead, because happiness is not your final destination. It can be the key to your legend.

SHORTCUT vol. 8- DOCTORS -100
BY Dr. BAK NGUYEN

If healing was the first step to your destiny and powers, there is a science to healing. Those with that science are doctors, the healers of the world. In India, healers are second only to the Gods! In SHORTCUT 170 DOCTOR QUOTES, Dr. Bak is dedicating the 8th volume of the series to his peers, doctors, from all around the world. Doctors too, have to walk their Quest of Identity, to heal from their pain and to walk their legend. Doctors need to heal and rejuvenate to keep healing the world. If healing is their science, in SHORTCUT, they will access the power of leveraging.

SUCCESS IS A CHOICE -060
BLUEPRINTS FOR HEALTH PROFESSIONALS
BY Dr. BAK NGUYEN

In SUCCESS IS A CHOICE, FINANCIAL MILLIONAIRE BLUEPRINTS FOR HEALTH PROFESSIONALS, Dr. Bak is breaking down the strategy to success for all those wearing white coats and scrubs: doctors, dentists, pharmacists, chiropractors, nurses, etc. Success is broken down into three key strategies: Financial Leverage - Compressing time - Always being in control. Presented by MILLION DOLLAR MINDSET, the book is covering more than the ways to create wealth, but also how to reach happiness and live a life without regrets. Dr. Bak is a successful cosmetic dentist with nearly 20 years of experience. He founded Mdex & Co, a company with the promise of reforming the whole dental industry for the better. While doing so, he discovered a passion for writing and for sharing. Multiple times World Record, Dr. Bak is writing a book every 2 weeks for the last 30 months. This is his 60th book, and he is still practicing. How he does it, is what he is sharing with us, SUCCESS, HAPPINESS, and mostly FREEDOM to all Health Professionals.

SYMPHONY OF SKILLS -001
BY Dr. BAK NGUYEN

You will enlighten the world with your potential. I can't wait to see all the differences that you will have in our world. Remember that power comes with responsibility. We can feel in his presence, a genuine force, a depth of energy, confidence, innocence, courage, and intelligence. Bak is always looking for answers, morning and night, he wants to understand the why and the why not. This book is the essence of the man. Dr. Bak is a force of nature who bears proudly his title eHappy. The man never ceases smiling and spreading his good vibe wherever he passes. He is not trapped in the nostalgia of the past nor the satisfaction of the present, he embodies the joy of what's possible, and what's to come. The more we read, the more we share, and we live. That is Bak, he charms us to evolve and to share his points of view, and before we know it, we are walking by his side, a journey we never saw coming.

T

THE 90 DAYS CHALLENGE -061
BY Dr. BAK NGUYEN

THE 90 DAYS CHALLENGE, is Dr. Bak's journey into the unknown. Overachiever writing 2 books a month on average, for the last 30 months, ambitious CEO, Industries' Disruptor, Dr. Bak seems to have success in everything he touches. Everything except the control of his weight. For nearly 20 years, he struggles with an overweight problem. Every time he scored big, he added on a little more weight. Well, this time, he exposes himself out there, in real-time and without filter, accepting the challenge of his brother-in-law, DON VO to lose 45 pounds within 90 days. That's half a pound a day, for three months. He will have to do so while keeping all of his other challenges on track, writing books at a world record pace, leading the dental industry into the new ERA, and keep seeing his patients. Undoubtedly entertaining, this is the journey of an ALPHA who simply won't give up. But this time, nothing is sure.

THE BOOK OF LEGENDS -024
BY Dr. BAK NGUYEN & WILLIAM BAK

The Book of Legends vol. 1 is the story behind the world record of Dr. Bak and his son, William Bak. All Dr. Bak had in mind was to keep his promise of writing a book with his son. They ended up writing 8 children's books within a month, scoring a new world record. William is also the youngest author having published in two languages. Those are world records waiting to be confirmed. History will say: to celebrate a first world record (writing 15 books / 15 months), for the love of his son, he will have scored a second world record: to write 8 books within a month! THE BOOK OF LEGENDS vol. 1 This is both a magical journey for both a father and a son looking to connect and find themselves. Join Dr. Bak and William Bak in their journey and their love for Life!

THE BOOK OF LEGENDS 2 -041
BY Dr. BAK NGUYEN & WILLIAM BAK

THE BOOK OF LEGENDS vol. 2 is the sequel of "CINDERELLA" but a true story between a father and his son. Together they have discovered a bond and a way to connect. The first BOOK OF LEGENDS covered the time of the first four books they wrote together within a month. The second BOOK OF LEGENDS is covering what happened after the curtains dropped, and what happened after reality kicked back in. If the first volume was about a fairy tale in vacation time, the second volume is about making it last in real Life. Share their journey and their love of Life!

THE BOOK OF LEGENDS 3 -086
THE END OF THE INNOCENCE AGE
BY Dr. BAK NGUYEN & WILLIAM BAK

THE BOOK OF LEGENDS 3 is a long work extending to almost 3 years. If the shocking duo known as Dr. Bak and prodigy William Bak has marked the imaginary writing world record upon world record, the story is not all pink. After the franchise of the CHICKEN BOOKS, William, now in his pre-teen years, wants to move away from the chicken tales. After 22 chicken books, a break is well deserved. that said, what is next? Both father and son thought that if they could do it once easily, they could do it again! They couldn't be any further from the truth. For 2 years, they were stuck in the quest for their next franchise of books. THE BOOK OF LEGENDS 3 started right around the end of the chicken franchise and would have ended with a failure if the book was to be released on time, the holiday season of that year. It took the duo another year to complete their story to add the last chapters of this book, hoping to end with a happy ending. Unfortunately, not all story ends the way we wish… this is the dark tome of the series, where the imagination got eclipsed. Follow William and Dr. Bak in their fight to keep the magic and connection alive.

THE CONFESSION OF A LAZY OVERACHIEVER -089
REINVENT YOURSELF FROM ANY CRISIS
BY Dr. BAK NGUYEN

In THE CONFESSION OF A LAZY OVERACHIEVER, Dr. Bak is opening up to his new marketing officer, Jamie, fresh out of school. She is young, full of energy, and looking to chill and still have it all. True to his character, Dr. Bak is giving Jamie some leeway to redefine Dr. Bak's brand to her demographic, the Millennials. This journey is about Dr. Bak satisfying the Millennials and answering their true questions in life. A rebel himself, his ambition to change the world started back on campus, some 25 years ago… then, life caught up with him. It took Dr. Bak 20 years to shake down the burdens of life, spread his wings free from Conformity, and start Overachieving. Doctor, CEO, and world record author, here is what Dr. Bak would have loved to know 25 years ago as was still on campus. In a word, this is cheating your way to success and freedom. And yes, it is possible. Success, Money, and Freedom, they all start with a mindset and the awareness of Time. Welcome to the Alphas.

THE ENERGY FORMULA -053
BY Dr. BAK NGUYEN

THE ENERGY FORMULA is a book dedicated to helping each individual to find the means to reach their purpose and goal in Life. Dr. Bak is a philosopher, a strategist, a business, an artist, and a dentist, how does he do all of that? He is doing so while mentoring proteges and leading the modernization of an entire industry. Until now, Momentum and Speed were the powers that he was building on and from. But those powers come from somewhere too. From a guide of our Quest of Identity, he became an ally in everyone's journey for happiness. THE ENERGY FORMULA is the book revealing step by step, the logic of building the right mindset and the way to ABUNDANCE and HAPPINESS, universally. It is not just a HOW TO book, but one that will change your life and guide you to the path of ABUNDANCE.

THE MODERN WOMAN -070
TO HAVE IT HAVE WITH NO SACRIFICE
BY Dr. BAK NGUYEN & Dr. EMILY LETRAN

In THE MODERN WOMAN: TO HAVE IT ALL WITH NO SACRIFICE, Dr. Bak joins forces with Dr. Emily Letran to empower all women to fulfill their desires, goals, and ambition. Both overachievers going against the odds, they are sharing their experience and wisdom to help all women to find confidence and support to redefine their lives. Dr. Emily Letran is a doctor in dentistry, an entrepreneur, author, and CERTIFIED HIGH-PERFORMANCE coach. For an Asian woman, she made it through the norms and the red tapes to find her voice. As she learnt and grew with mentors, today she is sharing her secret with the energy that will motivate all of the female genders to stand for what they deserve. Alpha doctor, Bak is joining his voice and perspective since this is not about gender equality, but about personal empowerment and the quest of Identity of each, man and woman. Once more, Dr. Bak is bringing LEVERAGE and REASON to the new social deal between man and woman. This is not about gender, but about confidence.

THE POWER BEHIND THE ALPHA -008
BY TRANIE VO & Dr. BAK NGUYEN

It's been said by a "great man" that "We are born alone and we die alone." Both men and women proudly repeat those words as wisdom since. I apologize in advance, but what a fat LIE! That's what I learnt and discovered in life since my mind and heart got liberated from the burden of scars and the ladders of society. I can have it all, not all at the same time, but I can have everything I put my mind and heart into. Actually, it is not completely true. I can have most of what I and Tranie put our minds into. Together, when we feel like one, there isn't much out of our reach. If I'm the mind, she's the heart; if I'm the Will, she's the means. Synergy is the core of our power. Tranie's aim is always Happiness. In Tranie's definition of life, there are no justifications, no excuses, no tomorrow. For Tranie, Happiness is measured by the minutes of every single day. This is why she's so strong and can heal people around her. That may also be why she doesn't need to talk much, since talking about the past or the future is, in her mind, dimming down the magic of the present, the Now. We both respect and appreciate that we are the whole balancing each other's equation of life, of love, of success. I was the plus and the minus, then I became the multiplication factor and grew into the exponential. And how is Tranie evolving in all of this? She is and always will be the balance. If anything, she is the equal sign of each equation.

THE POWER OF Dr. -066
THE MODERN TITLE OF NOBILITY
BY Dr. BAK NGUYEN, Dr. PAVEL KRASTEV AND COLLABORATORS

In THE POWER OF Dr., independent thinkers mean to exchange ideas. An idea can be very powerful if supported by a great work ethic. Work ethic, isn't that the main fabric of our white coats, scrubs, and title? In an era post-COVID where everything has been rebooted and that's the healthcare industry is facing its own fate: to evolve or to be replaced, Dr. Bak and Dr. Pavel reveal the source of their power and their playbook to move forward, ahead. The power we all hold is our resilience and discipline. We put that for years at the service of our profession, from a surgical perspective. Now, we can harness that same power to rewrite the rules, the industry, and our future. Post-COVID, the rules are being rewritten, will you be part of the team or left behind? "You can be in control!" More than personal growth and a motivational book, THE POWER OF Dr. is an awakening call to the doctor you look at when you graduate, with hope, with honour, with determination.

THE POWER OF YES -010
VOLUME ONE: IMPACT
BY Dr. BAK NGUYEN

In THE POWER OF YES, Dr. Bak is sharing his journey, opening up and embracing the world, one day at a time, one task at a time, one wish at a time. Far from a dare, saying YES allowed Dr. Bak to rewrite his mindset and break all the boundaries. This book is not one written in a few days or weeks, but the accumulation of a journey for 12 months. The journey started as Dr. Bak said YES to his producer to go on stage and speak... That YES opened a world of possibilities. Dr. Bak embraced each and every one of them. 12 months later, he is celebrating the new world record of writing 9 books written over a period of 12 months. To him, it will be a miss, missing the 12 on 12 mark. To the rest of the world, they just saw the birth of a force of nature, the Alpha force. THE

POWER OF YES is comprised of all the introductions of the adult books written by Dr. Bak within the first 12 months. Chapter by chapter, you can walk in his footstep seeing and smelling what he has. This is reality-literature with a twist of POWER. THE POWER OF YES! Discover your potential and your power. This is the POWER OF YES, volume one. Welcome to the Alphas.

THE POWER OF YES 2 -037
VOLUME TWO: SHAPELESS
BY Dr. BAK NGUYEN

In THE POWER OF YES, volume 2, Dr. Bak is continuing his journey, discovering his powers and influence. After 12 months of embracing the world by saying YES, he rose as an emerging force: he's been recognized as an INDUSTRIES DISRUPTOR, got nominated ERNST AND YOUNG ENTREPRENEUR OF THE YEAR, wrote 9 books within 12 months while launching the most ambitious private endeavour to reform his own industry, the dental field. Contender too many WORLD RECORDS, Dr. Bak is doing all of that in parallel. And yes, he is sleeping his nights and yes, he is writing his book himself, from the screen of his iPhone! Far from satisfied, Dr. Bak missed the mark of writing 12 books within 12 months. While everything is taking shape, everything could also crumble down at each turn. Now that Dr. Bak understands his powers, he is looking to test them and push them to their limits, looking to keep scoring world records while materializing his vision and enterprises. This is the awakening of a Force of Nature looking to change the world for the better while having fun sharing. Welcome to the Alphas.

THE POWER OF YES 3 -046
VOLUME THREE: LIMITLESS
BY Dr. BAK NGUYEN

In THE POWER OF YES, volume 3, the journey of Dr. Bak continues where the last volume left, in front of 300 plus people showing up to his first solo event, a Dr. Bak's event. On stage and in this book, Dr. Bak reveals how 12 months of saying YES to everything changed his life… actually, it was 18 months. From a dentist looking to change the world from a dental chair into a multiple times world record author, the journey of openness is a rendezvous with Fate. Dr. Bak is sharing almost in real-time his journey, and experiences, but above all, his feelings, doubts, and comebacks. From one book to the next, from one journey to the next, follow the adventure of a man looking to find his name, his worth, and his place in the world. Doing so, he is touching people Doing so, he is touching people and initiating their rise. Are you ready for more? Are you ready to meet your Fate and Destiny? Welcome to the Alphas.

THE POWER OF YES 4 -087
VOLUME FOUR: PURPOSE
BY Dr. BAK NGUYEN

In THE POWER OF YES, volume 4, the journey continues days after where the last volume left. After setting the new world record of writing 48 books within 24 months, Dr. Bak is not ready to stop. As volume one covers 12 months of journey, volume 2 covers 6 months. Well, volume 3 covers 4 months. The speed is building up and increasing, steadily. This is volume 4, RISING, after breaking the sound barrier. Dr. Bak has reached a state where he is above most resistance and friction, he is now in a universe of his own, discovering his powers as he walks his journeys. This is no fiction story or wishful thinking, THE POWER OF YES is the journey of Dr. Bak, from one world record to the next, from one book to the next. You too can walk your own legend, you just need to listen to your innersole and open up to the opportunity. May you get inspiration from the legendary journey of Dr. Bak and find your own Destiny. Welcome to the Alphas.

THE RISE OF THE UNICORN -038
BY Dr. BAK NGUYEN & Dr. JEAN DE SERRES

In THE RISE OF THE UNICORN, Dr. Bak is joining forces with his friend and mentor, Dr. Jean De Serres. Together both men had many achievements in their respective industries, but the advent of eHappyPedia, THE RISE OF THE UNICORN is a personal project dear to both of them: the QUEST OF HAPPINESS and its empowerment. This book is a special one since you are witnessing the conversation between two entrepreneurs looking to change the world by building unique tools and media. Just like any enterprise, the ride is never a smooth one in the park on a beautiful day. But this is about eHappyPedia, it is about happiness, right? So it will happen and with a smile attached to it! The unique value of this book is that you are sharing the ups and downs of the launch of a Unicorn, not just the glory of the fame, but also the doubts and challenges along the way. May it inspire you on your own journey to success and happiness.

THE RISE OF THE UNICORN 2 -076
eHappyPedia
BY Dr. BAK NGUYEN & Dr. JEAN DE SERRES

This is 2 years after starting the first tome. Dr. Bak's brand is picking up, between the accumulation of records and recognition. eHappyPedia is now hot for a comeback. In THE RISE OF THE UNICORN 2, Dr. Bak is retracing and addressing each of Dr. Jean De Serres' concerns about the weakness of the first version of eHappyPedia and the eHappy movement. This is the sort of creation and a UNICORN both in finance and in psychology. Never before, have you assisted in such a daily and decision-making process of a world phenomenon and of a company. Dr. Bak and Dr. De Serres are literally using the process of writing this series of books to plan and brainstorm the birth of a bluechip. More than an intriguing story, this is the journey of 2 experienced entrepreneurs changing the world.

THE U.A.X STORY -072
THE ULTIMATE AUDIO EXPERIENCE
BY Dr. BAK NGUYEN

This is the story of the ULTIMATE AUDIO EXPERIENCE, U.A.X. Follow Dr. Bak's footsteps in how he invented a new way to read and learn. Dr. Bak brings his experience as a movie producer and a director to elevate the reading experience to another level with entertaining value and make it accessible to everyone, auditive, and visual people alike.

After three years plus of research and development, and countless hours of trials and errors, Dr. Bak finally solved his puzzle: having written more than 1.1 million words. The irony is that he does not like to read, he likes audiobooks! U.A.X. finally allowed the opening of Dr. Bak's entire library to a new genre and media. U.A.X. is the new way to learn and enjoy Audiobooks. Made to be entertaining while keeping the self-educational value of a book, U.A.X. will appeal to both auditive and visual people. U.A.X. is the blockbuster of Audiobooks. The format has already been approved by iTunes, Amazon, Spotify, and all major platforms for global distribution and streaming.

THE VACCINE -077
BY Dr. BAK NGUYEN & WILLIAM BAK

In THE VACCINE, A TALE OF SPIES AND ALIENS, Dr. Bak reprises his role as mentor to William, his 10-year-old son, both as co-author and as doctor. William is living through the COVID war and has accumulated many, many questions. That morning, they got out all at once. From a conversation between father and son, Dr. Bak is making science into words keeping the interest of his son on a Saturday morning in bed. William is not just an audience, he is responsible to map the field with his questions. What started as a morning conversation between father and son, became within the next hour, a great project, their 23rd book together. Learn about the virus, and vaccination while entertaining your kids.

TIMING - TIME MANAGEMENT ON STEROIDS -074
BY Dr. BAK NGUYEN & WILLIAM BAK

In TIMING, TIME MANAGEMENT ON STEROIDS, Dr. Bak is sharing his secret to keep overachieving, and overdelivering while raising the bar higher and higher. We all have 24 hours in a day, so how can some do so much more than others? Dr. Bak is not only sharing his secrets and mindset about time and efficiency, he is literally living his own words as this book is written within his last sprint to set the next world record of writing 100 books within 4 years, with only 31 days to go. With 8 books to write in 31 days, that's a little less than 4 days per book! Share the journey of a man surfing the change and looking to see where is the limit of the human mind, writing. In the meantime, understand his leverage, mindset, and secrets to challenge your own limits and dreams.

TO OVERACHIEVE EVERYTHING BEING LAZY -090
CHEAT YOUR WAY TO SUCCESS
BY Dr. BAK NGUYEN

In TO OVERACHIEVE EVERYTHING BEING LAZY, Dr. Bak retakes his role talking to the millennials, the next generation. If in the first tome of the series LAZY, Dr. Bak addresses the general audience of millennials, especially young women, he is dedicating this tome to the ALPHA amongst the millennials, those aiming for the moon and looking, not only to be happy but to change the world. This is not another take on how to cheat your way to success or how to leverage laziness, but this is the recipe to build overachievers and rainmakers. For the young leaders with ambitions and talent, understanding TIME and ENERGY are crucial from your first steps in writing your our legend. If Dr. Bak had the chance to do it all over again, this is how he would do it! Welcome to the Alphas.

TORNADO -067
FORCE OF CHANGE
BY Dr. BAK NGUYEN

In TORNADO - FORCE OF CHANGE Dr. Bak is writing solo. In the midst of the COVID war, change is not a good intention anymore. Change, constant change has become a new reality, a new norm. From somebody who holds the title of Industries' Disruptor, how does he yield change to stay in control? Well, the changes from the COVID war are constant fear and much loss of individual liberty. Some can endure the change, some will ride it. Dr. Bak is sharing his angle of navigating the changes, yielding the improvisations, and to reinvent the goals, the means to stay relevant. From fighting to keep his companies Dr. Bak went on to let go of the uncontrollable to embrace the opportunity, he reinvented himself to ride the change and create opportunities from an unprecedented crisis. This is the story of a man refusing to kneel and accept defeat, smiling back at faith to find leverage and hope.

TOUCHSTONE -073
LEVERAGING TODAY'S PSYCHOLOGICAL SMOG
BY Dr. BAK NGUYEN & Dr. KEN SEROTA

TOUCHSTONE, LEVERAGING TODAY'S PSYCHOLOGICAL SMOG is mapping to navigate and thrive in today's high and constant stress environment. After 40 years in practice, Dr. Serota is concerned about the evolution of the career of health care professionals and the never-ending level of stress. What is stress, and what are its effects, damages, and symptoms? If COVID-19 revealed to the world that we are fragile, it also revealed most of the broken and the flaws of our system. For now a century, dentistry has been a champion in depression, Drug addiction, and suicide rates, and the curve is far from flattening. Dr. Bak is sharing his perspective and experience dealing with stress and how to leverage it into a constructive force. From the stress of a doctor with no right to failure to the stress of an entrepreneur never knowing the future, Dr. Bak is sharing his way to use stress as leverage.

ABOUT THE AUTHORS

From Canada, **Dr. BAK NGUYEN**, Nominee Ernst and Young Entrepreneur of the year, Grand Homage Lys DIVERSITY, LinkedIn & TownHall Achiever of the year and TOP 100 Doctors 2021. Dr. Bak is a cosmetic dentist, CEO and founder of Mdex & Co. His company is revolutionizing the dental field.

Speaker and motivator, he holds the world record of writing 100 books in 4 years accumulating many world records (to be officialized). Before that, he held the world record of writing 9 books over 12 months, then, 15 books within 15 months to set the bar even higher with the world record of 36 books written within 18 months + 1 week.

By his second author anniversary, he scored his new landmark world record of 48 books within 24 months. And then 72 books in 36 months. By the 4th anniversary, Dr. Bak scored his usual landmark of writing 96 books over 48 months, but he pushed even further, scoring also the new world record of 100 books written within 4 years!

His books are covering:

- **ENTREPRENEURSHIP**
- **LEADERSHIP**
- **QUEST OF IDENTITY**
- **DENTISTRY AND MEDICINE**
- **PARENTING**
- **CHILDREN BOOKS**
- **PHILOSOPHY**

In 2003, he founded Mdex, a dental company upon which in 2018, he launched the most ambitious private endeavour to reform the dental industry, Canada-wide. Philosopher, he has close to his heart the quest of happiness of the people surrounding him, patients and colleagues alike. In 2020, he launched an International collaborative initiative named **THE ALPHAS** to share knowledge and for Entrepreneurs and Doctors to thrive through the Greatest Pandemic and Economic depression of our time.

In 2016, he co-found with Tranie Vo, Emotive World Incorporated, a tech research company to use technology to empower happiness and sharing. U.A.X. the ultimate audio experience is the landmark project on which the team is advancing, utilizing the technics of the movie industry and the advancement in ARTIFICIAL INTELLIGENCE to save the book industry and upgrade the continuing education space.

These projects have allowed Dr. Nguyen to attract interest from the international and diplomatic community and he is now the centre of a global discussion on the wellbeing and the future of the health profession. It is in that matter that he shares his thoughts and encourages the health community to share their own stories.

"It's not worth it to go through it alone! Together, we stand, alone, we fall."

Motivational speaker and serial entrepreneur, philosopher and author, in his own words, Dr. Nguyen describes himself as a dentist by circumstances, an entrepreneur by nature and a communicator by passion.

He also holds recognitions from the Canadian Parliament and the Canadian Senate.

From Canada, **ANDRÉ CHATELAIN** acts as a Business Consultant and offers coaching services for managers and senior executives. In addition, he contributes, with the Université de Sherbrooke, to the development of training programs for 2nd cycle companies and students. He also sits on a few Boards of Directors. Until September 3, 2017, he was Senior Vice-President, Personal Services, Payment and Marketing at Desjardins Group. His mandate was to develop and deploy banking and financing for retail clients, as well as payment solutions for the Desjardins group. Its teams are also responsible for marketing activities for individual clients and marketing activities for all clienteles in Quebec.

Transversally, as first vice-president, he also managed the Desjardins brand and ensured the alignment and cohesion of Desjardins' actions in terms of marketing, marketing to members and customers' experience in all distribution channels. Mr. Chatelain worked for Desjardins Group for 28 years. During these years, he held various positions in the areas of corporate finance, business development, risk management, marketing, operational efficiency and strategic planning.

He has also held several management positions, including Vice-President Risk Management, Vice-President Marketing – Business and, more recently, Senior Vice-President and General Manager of Desjardins Card Services. Mr. Chatelain has served on several boards internally and externally with Desjardins Group.He holds a Master of Business Administration (MBA) from the Université de Sherbrooke and a Bachelor of Administration (BAA concentration finance) from the Université du Québec en Outaouais.

From Canada, **FRANÇOIS DUFOUR** has been an entrepreneur and a marketer all of his life. Throughout his career, he has always been the one asking the hard questions to himself and his contemporaries to better understand societal and economic mechanisms. He has obtained a bachelor's degree in economics from Bishop's University, a Master of Science from ESCEM-Poitiers and a master's in business (International Management) from Sherbrooke University.

From Canada, **TRANIE VO** is the co-founder and COO of Mdex & Co, a management company in the health sector. Graduated from McGill University with a bachelor degree in mechanical engineering, she co-found the company which she built from the ground up for the last 20 years. She is a veteran entrepreneur embodying woman's leadership and the diversity movement of the leader class. She co-wrote a book with her partner, Dr. Bak Nguyen on the balance to maintain between being a leader and a woman, standing behind her man.

In 2020, with her determination and resilience, she inspired the creation of the international organization of thinkers and difference makers known as THE ALPHAS.

From Canada, **William Bak** is a 12 years old prodigy. At the age of 8 years old, he co-wrote a series of chicken books with his dad, Dr. Bak. Together, they are changing the world, one mind at a time, writing books for kids. So far, they have 32 books together.

He co-wrote the 11 chicken books in ENGLISH and then, had to translate his own books in FRENCH. This is how he has 22 chicken books. William also co-wrote 4 parenting books with his dad, Dr. Bak, THE BOOK OF LEGENDS volumes 1, 2 and 3. The 4th volume started a new trilogy named THE RISE OF LEGENDS; the first volume of THE RISE OF LEGENDS; 2 Vaccine books (French and English); TIMING, William's first Apollo Protocol book. Lately, William has also written his first book solo at the age of 11, PAPA, J'SUIS PAS CON and the PROLOGUES OF DESTINY, volumes 1 and 2, and AU PAYS DES PAPAS 1 and 2.

To promote his books, William embraced the stage for the first time in 2019 talking to a crowd of 300+ people. Since he has appeared in many videos to talk about his books and upcoming projects. In the midst of COVID, he got bored and started his YOUTUBE CHANNEL: GAMEBAK, reviewing video games. By the end of 2020, he has joined THE ALPHAS as the youngest anchor of the upcoming world project COVIDCONOMICS in which he will give his perspective and host the opinions of his generation.

> "I will show you. I won't force you. But I won't wait for you."
> - William Bak and Dr. Bak

Writing with his Dad, William holds world records to be officialized: the youngest author writing in 2 languages, co-author of 8 books within a month, the first kid to have written 20 children's books, the child to have written his first solo book in 9 days, the first child who wrote 36 books within 45 months.

UAX

ULTIMATE AUDIO EXPERIENCE

A new way to learn and enjoy Audiobooks. Made to be entertaining while keeping the self-educational value of a book, UAX will appeal to both auditive and visual people. UAX is the blockbuster of Audiobooks.

UAX will cover most of Dr. Bak's books and is now negotiating to bring more authors and more titles to the UAX concept. Now streaming on Spotify, Apple Music and Amazon Prime. Available for download on all major music platforms. Give it a try today!

AMAZON - BARNES & NOBLE - APPLE BOOKS - KINDLE
SPOTIFY - APPLE MUSIC

C O M B O

PAPERBACK/AUDIOBOOK

ACTIVATION

Please register your book to receive the link to your audiobook version. Register at:
https://drbaknguyen.com/covidconomics-inflation-registry

FROM THE SAME AUTHOR
Dr. Bak Nguyen

TITLES AVAILABLE AT
www.Dr.BakNguyen.com

MAJOR LEAGUES' ACCESS

FACTEUR HUMAIN -035
LE LEADERSHIP DU SUCCÈS
par Dr. BAK NGUYEN & CHRISTIAN TRUDEAU

THE RISE OF THE UNICORN -038
BY Dr. BAK NGUYEN & Dr. JEAN DE SERRES

CHAMPION MINDSET -039
LEARNING TO WIN
BY Dr. BAK NGUYEN & CHRISTOPHE MULUMBA

THE RISE OF THE UNICORN 2 -076
eHappyPedia
BY Dr. BAK NGUYEN & Dr. JEAN DE SERRES

BRANDING -044
BALANCING STRATEGY AND EMOTIONS
BY Dr. BAK NGUYEN

BUSINESS

SYMPHONY OF SKILLS -001
BY Dr. BAK NGUYEN

LA SYMPHONIE DES SENS -002
ENTREPREUNARIAT
par Dr. BAK NGUYEN

INDUSTRIES DISRUPTORS -006
BY Dr. BAK NGUYEN

CHANGING THE WORLD FROM A DENTAL
CHAIR -007
BY Dr. BAK NGUYEN

THE POWER BEHIND THE ALPHA -008
BY TRANIE VO & Dr. BAK NGUYEN

SELFMADE -036
GRATITUDE AND HUMILITY
BY Dr. BAK NGUYEN

THE U.A.X STORY -072
THE ULTIMATE AUDIO EXPERIENCE
BY Dr. BAK NGUYEN

CRYPTOCONOMICS 101 - TO COME
MY PERSONAL JOURNEY
FROM 50K TO 1 MILLION
BY Dr. BAK NGUYEN

CHILDREN'S BOOK
with William Bak

The Trilogy of Legends

THE LEGEND OF THE CHICKEN HEART -016
LA LÉGENDE DU COEUR DE POULET -017
BY Dr. BAK NGUYEN & WILLIAM BAK

PARENTING

THE ORIGIN SERIES

PERSONAL GROWTH

THE ALPHA MASTERMIND FRANCHISE

THE LAZY FRANCHISE

PHILOSOPHY

SHORTCUT

SOCIETY

TEEN'S FICTION
with William Bak

LEGENDS OF DESTINY

THE POWER OF YES

THE POWER OF YES 5 -091
VOLUME FIVE: ALPHA
BY Dr. BAK NGUYEN

THE POWER OF YES 6 092
VOLUME SIX: PERSPECTIVE
BY Dr. BAK NGUYEN

TITRES DISPONIBLES AU

www.DrBakNguyen.com

AMAZON - BARNES & NOBLE - APPLE BOOKS - KINDLE
SPOTIFY - APPLE MUSIC

UNLIMITED ACCESS
DR. BAK'S ENTIRE AUDIO LIBRARY

Since Dr. Bak set his new landmark world record of writing 100 books in 4 years, he is opening his entire audio library, audiobooks and UAX albums, exclusively to all VIP members for $9.99/month.

By becoming a VIP member, you will have access to all Dr. Bak's audiobooks and UAX albums. Those are the ones today bought at Apple Books, Audible, and in COMBO version at Amazon. The UAX albums are those streaming on Apple Music, Spotify, and Amazon Prime Music.

As a VIP, you will also have prime access to the audiobooks as soon as they are completed, hitting them before they reach the mainstream outlets. Get your membership today!

http://drbaknguyen.com/members

Bienvenu(e)s aux Alphas.

DR.
Bak Nguyen

www.ingramcontent.com/pod-product-compliance
Lightning Source LLC
Chambersburg PA
CBHW061306220326
41599CB00026B/4758